W9-AHU-454

ഔ

This publication is designed to provide current information in regard to the resources and services in Rhode Island available to both seniors and disabled individuals, as well as their families, caregivers, and professionals involved in the care of seniors and disabled individuals. It is sold with the understanding that the publisher and author is not engaged in rendering legal or other professional services. If legal advice is required, the services of Laura M. Krohn can be sought privately by calling (401) 398-8383.

- Partially from a Declaration of Principles jointly adopted by a Committee of the American Bar Association and a Committee of Publishers and Associations.

ISBN No. 978-0-981-5005-1-5

Printed in the United States of America

Welcome to the second edition of the Rhode Island Senior Resource Guide, a comprehensive guide to senior services including healthcare providers, legal information, housing options, emergency services, as well as other valuable and educational resources. This compilation encompasses the physical, emotional, legal, financial and psychological aspects of finding and choosing appropriate care for your aged or disabled loved one.

I am confident this educational tool will help seniors, the disabled community, and their caregivers navigate through the often overwhelming number of resources available in Rhode Island.

In meeting the increasing needs of my clients, I have been fortunate enough to enjoy a rewarding and fulfilling career that extends beyond handling legal transactions.

I am grateful to be able to have spent the last decade practicing in the area of Elder Law. I have learned as much from my clients as they have learned from me!

Laura M. Krohn

To schedule an appointment with Laura please call:

401-398-8383

Laura M. Krohn Elder Law Attorney
Senior Resource Clinic
631 Main Street
East Greenwich, Rhode Island 02818

www.seniorguideri.com

From left, Laura M. Krohn, *Elder Law Attorney*,

Verna Luebeck and David Luebeck

Burrillville

Woonsocket

North
Smithfield

Cumberland

Central
Falls

Glocester

Smithfield

Lincoln

North
Providence

Pawtucket

Johnston

Providence

East
Providence

Foster

Scituate

Cranston

Barrington

Warren

West
Warwick

Warwick

Coventry

Bristol

West Greenwich

East
Greenwich

Portsmouth

Tiverton

Exeter

North
Kingstown

Jamestown

Middletown

Little
Compton

Hopkinton

Richmond

South
Kingstown

Newport

Narragansett

Charlestown

Westerly

Bristol County
Kent County
Newport County
Providence County
Washington County

New Shoreham

TABLE OF CONTENTS

The following Table of Contents for The Senior Resource Guide of Rhode Island has been carefully designed to assist you in finding resources for the elderly and disabled.

The resources have been placed in an order which takes into consideration typical priority of need. The evolution of need often begins with keeping seniors active in the community and in their homes for as long as possible and generally concludes with finding the appropriate level of care to keep seniors safe and provide them with the highest quality of life.

Table of Contents

TABLE OF CONTENTS

TABLE OF CONTENTS

SENIOR GUIDE RESOURCE KEY

Throughout this guide symbols are used to represent the various types of funding, services and amenities each establishment offers. Please refer to the key featured below to better understand this resource guide.

MA	MEDICAID
MW	MEDICAID WAIVER
VAA	VETERANS AID & ATTENDANCE
R	REHABILITATION
	RESPITE CARE
	SECURED UNIT
	CHAPEL
	FITNESS ROOM
	PETS
	SALON

STAYING AT HOME: AGING IN PLACE

HOME MODIFICATIONS

<u>Staying in Your Home as You Age</u>

<u>By Steve St Onge</u>

According to a recent AARP survey, the majority of seniors prefer to remain in their own homes for as long as possible. This trend is called 'Aging in Place'. But their homes, unless properly designed and equipped, will not be able to accommodate their changing levels of mobility, vision and needs.

Accessibility modifications allow people to remain in their homes as they age. *Amenities like walk-in showers, better lighting, grab rails, and other modifications allow seniors to live comfortably, safely and independently in their own home for as long as possible.*

Most homeowners don't wish to refer to their home as 'handicapped-accessible' - in fact, the industry term for this is now called 'Universal Design.' *This is a user-friendly approach to design where people of any age, size, and ability can live and move about the environment comfortably, safely and independently.* It incorporates such features as lever style door handles and faucets, accessible bathing facilities, adjustable or varying height sinks and countertops, wider doorways, and low thresholds - all using stylish products and techniques that avoid an institutional look.

The National Association of Home Builders (NAHB) and the AARP have developed a new designation called Certified Aging in Place Specialist (CAPS) to assist aging homeowners to identify reputable contractors that have been trained in Universal Design techniques and to understand the unique needs of our aging population. Staying at home is an option for aging seniors, especially if one plans ahead and makes the proper modifications to their homes.

To find a CAPS certified remodeler, go to www.NAHB.org and click on the CAPS link. *Steve St. Onge is a Certified Aging in Place Specialist (CAPS) and regularly speaks on the topic of Aging in Place and Universal Design. He can be reached at (401) 463-1550 or email him at Steve@RIKB.com*

Is A Reverse Mortgage Right For You?

If you're a homeowner age 62 or older, a reverse mortgage could be right for you. Use the cash to supplement your retirement income, finance home renovations, or pay for long-term health care coverage. *For whatever is important to you.*

A reverse mortgage is a loan that allows senior homeowners to convert home equity into cash while living at home for as long as they want to. You can receive payments as a lump sum, line of credit, or monthly payment for a specific term or for life. **Funds are tax-free can may be used for** any purpose. Borrowers continue to own their own home. There is no monthly mortgage payment, income or credit qualifications, and the loan does not becomes due until the (last) borrower moves out, dies or sells the home. Enjoy financial security and independence.

Reverse Mortgages "The Basics"

- A loan that allows homeowners, age 62 or older, to convert home equity into cash while living at home for as long as they want

- No income or full credit review

- Borrower can receive payments as a lump sum, line of credit, monthly payment for a specific term or for life. Funds are tax-free and can be used for any purpose

- Loan becomes due when the (last) borrower moves out, dies or sells the home

- Borrowers continue to own their own home

- *Home must be 1-4 family residence*

Reverse Mortgages "The Benefits"

- Allows assets to be liquidated without triggering tax events or requiring any debt service.

- Proceeds are not considered income and therefore are not taxable. Eligibility for Social Security or Medicare benefits are not affected.

3

- Loan is repaid at time of death, sale or move. Repayment never exceeds value of the home.

- Loan proceeds can be used for whatever is important to you.

- Independent counseling is required for all reverse mortgages

The "Borrowers Responsibility"

- Keep property taxes current

- Maintain homeowners insurance

- Maintain property in reasonable living condition

- Live in the home as primary residence

The 'safety of A Home Equity Conversion Mortgage (HECM)' Reverse mortgage

- Federal Housing Authority administers the Home Equity Conversion Mortgage and guarantees that the borrower receive their requested loan advance.

- The borrower(s) will never owe more than the fair market value of the home upon loan maturity

- You can change your payment distribution at any time during the life of the loan.

The "Typical Closing Costs"

- Origination fee (2% of home value)

- Third party closing cost (appraisal, credit report, flood certificate, attorney fees)

- Mortgage Insurance Premium (2% of home value)

- Most fees can be paid from loan proceeds

- *Closing costs may be dramatically reduced with the fixed rate products*

For more complete information about Reverse Mortgages, call Brenda Archambault, Reverse Mortgage Specialist at Washington Trust at 800-475-2265 x1220.

SUBSIDIZED HOUSING &HOUSING ASSISTANCE

Rhode Island Housing and Subsidized Housing

44 Washington Street

Providence, RI 02903

Telephone: (401) 457-1234; TTY: (401) 450-1394

Rhode Island Housing oversees the management of 20,000 apartment for low-income seniors, frail seniors, and person with disabilities. Approximately 15,000 of these apartment are Section 8. Under t his category, tenants pay 30 percent of their income for rent. Many cities and towns have public housing authorities that provide affordable apartments and Section 8 vouchers. The remaining 5,000 apartments have a variety of subsidies that keep the rents affordable for low-income households. Applicant can apply for housing in any community in which they would like to live. Be prepared to find out that most communities do have long waiting lists.

For a complimentary housing application for your city or town, please call Laura Krohn's Senior Resource Clinic at (401) 398-8383 and we will gladly mail one out to you for submission to the appropriate housing authority. For legal advice regarding the housing application, you will need to schedule a consultation with the attorney at the clinic.

Crossroads Rhode Island

www.crossroadsri.org

160 Broad Street

Providence, RI 02903

Telephone: (401) 521-2255; TTY: (401) 277-4381

Crossroads Rhode Island provides information and referrals for the homeless and those in transition.

Home Improvement Assistance & Lead Abatement Program

www.rhodeislandhousing.org

44 Washington Street

Providence, RI 02903

Telephone: (401) 450-1350

Rhode Island Housing's Home Improvement and Lead Abatement program can assist qualified residents in obtaining low-interest home repair and improvement loans.

- *There may also be grants or loans for home repairs available in your city or town. You should call your city or town housing authority or visit your town/city hall for more information.*

Operation Stand Down

www.osdri.org

1010 Hartford Avenue

Johnston, RI 02919

Telephone: (401) 383-4730

Operation Stand Down Rhode Island serves homeless and disabled veterans.

Rhode Island Coalition for the Homeless

www.rihomeless.org

160 Broad Street

Providence, RI 02903

Telephone: (401) 421-6458

The Rhode Island Coalition for the Homeless publishes he Street Sheet, a listing of emergency shelters, food pantries, and other resources.

HEATING ASSISTANCE

Low-Income Home Energy Assistance Program; LIHEAP

Heating assistance is available to households that are responsible for their own heating costs. The Low-Income Home Energy Assistance Program provides heating assistance to income eligible customers in meeting the costs of keeping their homes warm in the winter months.

The amount of assistance provided is based on household size and income level. Current income guidelines are as follows:

1-Person household income cap is $24,395

2-Person household income cap is $31,901

3-Person household income cap is $39,407

The following agencies can assist with applying for heating assistance (see communities served to locate which agency you should call):

Blackstone Valley Community Action Program

www.bvcap.org

32 Goff Avenue   Phone: (401) 723-0227

Pawtucket, RI 02860

Communities served: Central Falls, Cumberland, Lincoln, North Smithfield, Pawtucket, and Woonsocket.

*

Cranston Comprehensive Community Action Program

www.comcap.org

311 Doric Avenue   Phone: (401) 467-9610

Cranston, RI 02910

Communities served: Cranston, Foster, and Scituate.

Housing Assistance Continued....

East Bay Community Action Program

www.ebcap.org

100 Bullocks Point Avenue   Phone: (401) 437-5102

Riverside, RI 02915

Communities served: Barrington, Bristol, East Providence, Jamestown, Little Compton, Middletown, Newport, Portsmouth, Tiverton, and Warren .

*

Tri-Town Community Action Program

www.tri-town.org

1126 Hartford Avenue   Phone: (401) 351-2750

Johnston, RI 02919

Communities served: Burillville, Chepachet, Glocester, Johnston, and North Providence.

*

Providence Community Action Program

www.procapri.org

518 Hartford Avenue   Phone: (401) 273-2000

Providence, RI 02909

Communities served: Providence

*

South County Community Action Program

1935 Kingston Road   Phone: (401) 789-3016

Peace Dale, RI 02879   *www*.sccainc.org

Communities served: Charlestown, Exeter, Hopkinton, Narragansett, New Shoreham, North Kingstown, Richmond, South Kingstown, West Greenwich, and Westerly.

Heating Assistance Continued....

West Bay Community Action Program

*www.*westbaycap.org

208 Buttonwoods Avenue   Phone: (401) 732-4660

Warwick, RI 02886

Communities served: Coventry, East Greenwich, Warwick, and West Warwick.

*

Citizen's Energy

*www.*citizensenergy.com

The Citizen's Energy website provides a listing of energy assistance resources in Rhode Island.

*

Diocese of Providence

*www.*heatri.com

184 Broad Street   Phone: (401) 421-7833

Providence, RI 02903

The Diocese of Providence has a program call **_Keep the Heat On_** that provides heating assistance in emergency situations.

*

Salvation Army

www.use.salvationarmy.com

386 Broad Street   Phone: (401) 831-1119

Providence, RI 02903

The Salvation Army Rhode Island provides heating and utility assistance.

COMPANIONSHIP AT HOME

Neighborhood Friendly Visitor Program

184 Broad Street   Phone: (401) 421-7833 ext.4

Providence, RI 02903

The Neighborhood Friendly Visitor Program provides companionship and friendly support to individuals. Volunteers visit homebound individuals and offer the social contact every person needs in their life. The program welcomes volunteers who wish to volunteer some of their time to others. To find out about obtaining a visitor, simply call the numbers above.

Rhode Island's Senior Companion Program

The Senior Companion Program is sponsored by the Department of Elderly Affairs and is funded by the Corporation for National and Community Service. All volunteers are 60 and over, have limited income and receive a tax-free stipend and other benefits while serving clients 20 hours weekly.

The Volunteers serve isolated and older adults in their homes and other community sites, such as senior centers and adult day care centers. In an average wee, Senior Companions visit with almost 500 individuals, offering friendship and compassion to those in need.

Southern Rhode Island Volunteers: SRI

www.southernrivol.org

25 Saint Dominic Road   Phone: (401) 789-2362

Wakefield, RI 02879

Southern Rhode Island Volunteers, also known as Seniors Helping Others, offers a range of services such as visitation and education, that enrich the lives of those in need, while also enriching the lives of the volunteers and the entire community. Call or visit the website for more information.

LIFELINE PERSONAL EMERGENCY RESPONSE SYSTEMS

Lifeline clients are supported 24 hours a day, seven days a week, by wearing a communicator button. When the button is pressed, the client is connected the subscriber to a Lifeline operator. From there, the operator will assess the situation and contact the appropriate help.

Lifeline also offers special units for clients with visual and/or hearing impairments.

For more information or to order Lifeline, contact one of the following providers:

Care New England Home Health

Phone: (800) 242-1306

You can find more information about Lifeline at any of the Care New England affiliates, such as Butler, Kent Hospital, Women & Infants Hospital, and Care New England Wellness Centers. You can also contact Health Touch, a VNA of Care New England, at (800) 640-8434.

Homefront Health Care

Contact: Beverly Oleksy

Phone: (401) 738-0409

Toll-Free: (800) 242-1306 *4610

HEALTH WATCH EMERGENCY RESPONSE SYSTEMS

Health Watch Systems include the following safety features:

1. **The Daily Automatic System Self-test**: Automatically verifies the system is working every single day, with NO action needed from the subscriber.

2. **The Automatic Pendant Supervisor**: Automatically monitors the Alarm Transmitter Pendant all day long to check its battery status and condition to ensure it's working properly.

3. **Emergency Communication Mode:** Allows the Response Center operator to increase the volume of the system console's speaker and microphone to hear a person's voice — even if he or she is behind a closed door or in another room.

For more information or to order Health Watch, contact the following providers:

VNS of Greater Rhode Island

6 Blackstone Valley Place, Suite 515

Lincoln, RI 02865

Phone: (401) 769-5670

Toll-Free: (800) 696-7991 ext. 7439

Email: healthwatch@vnsgri.org

SENIOR
CONTINUING
EDUCATION
OPPORTUNITIES

EDCUATIONAL OPPORTUNITIES

The Elderhostel Program

The Elderhostel Program is the world's largest travel and education organization for persons age 55 and older. The organization's focus is on education and lifelong learning adventures. Financial assistance is available to eligible participants.

For more information call 1-877-426-8056 or visit www.elderhostel.org.

The Osher Lifelong Learning Institute

The Osher Lifelong Learning Institute at the University of Rhode Island is a learning community for adults age 50 and older. *Participants can explore a broad range of subjects and programs without the worry of exams, grades, or academic requirements!* There is a $50 inaugural membership fee.

For more information call (401) 874-5331 or (401) 864-7846 or visit www.uri.edu/OLLI

Rhode Island State Colleges and Universities

Rhode Island residents age 60 and over may take courses at state colleges and universities, without paying tuition, on a space-available basis. Students must meet the income guidelines and other fees may apply. Contact the college/university office of continuing education for more information.

You are Never Too Older to Learn

SENIOR
CENTERS

What Is a Senior Center?

Senior Centers are meeting places that are dedicated to helping seniors live meaningful lives of dignity, enjoyment and useful purpose. The centers' main focus is improving and enriching lives of seniors through programs, resources and volunteer work. They provide programs and services that enhance an individual's social, physical and mental well-being.

Each town typically has its own Senior Center for the surrounding community. Membership fees vary for town and non-town members but prices are generally minimal. Most centers provide their own transportation. Ask your community senior center for more specific transportation information.

Membership fees, hours, and availability of programs may vary by location. Call your center for more details and information. For your convenience, the following Senior Centers have been listed alphabetically by city/town.

Barrington:

Barrington Senior Center

www.CI.Barrington.RI.US

281 County Road   Phone: (401) 247-1926

Barrington, RI 02806   Fax: (401) 247-3790

Bristol:

Benjamin Church Senior Center

1020 Hope Street   Phone: (401) 253-8458

Bristol, RI 02809   Fax: (401) 253-8009

Central Falls:

Ralph J. Holden Community Center

361 Cowden Street   Phone: (401) 727-7425

Central Falls, RI 02863   Fax: (401) 727-7428

Charlestown:

Charlestown Community Center

www.CharlestownRI.org

Ninigret Park-Old Post Road

P.O. Box 1061   Phone: (401) 364-9955

Charlestown, RI 02813   Fax: (401) 364-0330

Coventry:

The Coventry Senior Center

www.Town.Coventry.RI.US

50 Wood Street   Phone: (401) 822-9175

Coventry, RI 02816   Fax: (401) 822-9128

Cranston:

The Cranston Department of Senior Services

www.CranstonRI.com

1070 Cranston Street   Phone: (401) 461-1000

Cranston, RI 02920   Fax: (401) 946-5909

Cumberland:

The Cumberland Senior Center

www.CumberlandRI.org

1464 Diamond Hill Road   Phone: (401) 334-2555

Cumberland, RI 02864   Fax: (401) 335-4473

East Greenwich:

East Greenwich Senior Services

125 Main Street   Phone: (401) 886-8669

East Greenwich, RI 02818   Fax: (401) 886-8623

East Providence:

The East Providence Senior Center

www.CityOfEastProv.com

610 Waterman Avenue

Phone: (401) 435-7800

East Providence, RI 02914

Fax: (401) 435-7803

Glocester:

Glocester Senior Center

www.GlocesterRI.org / SeniorServices.htm

1210 Putnam Pike

Phone: (401) 710-9860

Chepachet, RI 02815

Hopkinton:

Hopkinton Senior Services

www.HopkintonRI.org

Phone: (401) 377-7795

188A Main Street

Alternate: (401) 377-2857

Hopkinton, RI 02804

Fax: (401) 377-7756

Jamestown:

Jamestown Senior Center

6 West Street

Phone: (401) 423-2658

Jamestown, RI 02835

Fax: (401) 423-3252

Johnston:

Johnston Senior Center

1291 Hartford Avenue

Phone: (401) 944-3343

Johnston, RI 02919

Fax: (401) 944-3560

Lincoln:

The Lincoln Senior Center

www.LincolnRI.org

40 Chapel Street

Lincoln, RI 02865

Phone: (401) 723-3270

Fax: (401) 723-4344

Middletown:

The Middletown Senior Center

www.MiddletownRI.com / Senior

650 Green End Avenue

Middletown, RI 02842

Phone: (401) 849-8823

Fax: (401) 845-0411

Narragansett:

Narragansett Community Center

www.NarragansettRI.com

53 Mumford Road

Narragansett, RI 02882

Phone: (401) 782-0675

Fax: (401) 788-2565

Newport:

Edward King House

www.EdwardKingHouse.com

35 King Street

Newport, RI 02840

Phone: (401) 846-7426

Martin Luther King Center

www.MLKccenter.org

20 West Broadway   Phone: (401) 846-4828

Newport, RI 02840   Fax: (401) 848-7360

North Kingstown:

Beechwood House Senior Center

www.NorthKingstown.org/senior

10 Beach Street   Phone: (401) 294-3331

North Kingstown, RI 02852   Fax: (401) 294-3020

North Providence:

Salvatore Mancini Center

www.smrac.com

2 Atlantic Boulevard   Phone: (401) 231-0742

North Providence, RI 02911   Fax: (401) 232-3460

Pawtucket:

Leon Mathieu Senior Center

Email: Mathieuctr@yahoo.com

420 Main Street   Phone: (401) 728-7582

Pawtucket, RI 02860   Fax: (401) 725-8220

Portsmouth:

The Portsmouth Multi Purpose Senior Center

www.PortsmouthRI.com

110 Bristol Ferry Road   Phone: (401) 683-4106

Portsmouth, RI 02871   Fax: (401) 683-4001

Providence:

DaVinci Community Center

www.DavinciCenter.org

470 Charles Street   Phone: (401) 272-7474

Providence, RI 02904   Fax: (401) 272-7960

Elmwood Community Center

www.ElmwoodCommunityCenter.org

155 Niagra Street   Phone: (401) 654-4960

Providence, RI 02907   Fax: (401) 941-2618

Federal Hill Community Center

9 Courtland Street   Phone: (401) 421-4722

Providence, RI 02909   Fax: (401) 421-4725

Fox Point Senior Center

90 Ives Street   Phone: (401)751-2217

Providence, RI 02906   Fax: (401) 751-2217

Hamilton House

www.HistoricHamilton.com

276 Angell Street   Phone: (401) 831-1800

Providence, RI 02906

Hartford Park Senior Center

20 Syracuse Street

Providence, RI 02909

Jewish Community Center

www.jccri.org / seniors

401 Elmgrove Avenue   Phone: (401) 861-8800

Providence, RI 02906   Fax: (401) 861-8806

Nickerson House Senior Center

133 Delaine Street   Phone: (401) 351-2241

Providence, RI 02909   Fax: (401) 272-3296

Silver Lake Center

529 Plainfield Street   Phone: (401) 944-8300

Providence, RI 02909   Fax: (401) 946-3260

St. Martin DePorres Senior Center

160 Cranston Street   Phone: (401) 274-6783

Providence, RI 02907   Fax: (401) 274-5930

Washington Park Community Center

42 Jillson Street   Phone: (401) 461-6650

Providence, RI 02905   Fax: (401) 781-5262

West End Community Center

109 Bucklin Street   Phone: (401) 781-4242

Providence, RI 02907   Fax: (401) 467-7990

Westminster Senior Center

133 Matthewson Street   Phone: (401) 274-6900

Providence, RI 02903   Fax: (401) 453-1149

Richmond:

Richmond Adult Center

1168 Main Street   Phone: (401) 539-6144

Richmond, RI 02898   Fax: (401) 491-9363

Scituate:

Scituate Senior Center

www.ScituateRI.org

1315 Chopmist Hill Road   Phone: (401) 647-2662

North Scituate, RI 02857   Fax: (401) 647-3160

Smithfield:

Smithfield Senior Center

www.SmithfieldRI.com/SeniorCenter.htm

1 William Hawkins, Jr. Trail   Phone: (401) 949-4590

Smithfield, RI 02828   Fax: (401) 949-4593

South Kingstown:

The Center

www.SouthKingstownRI.com

25 Saint Dominic Road   Phone: (401) 789-0268

Wakefield, RI 02879   Fax: (401) 782-1223

Tiverton:

Tiverton Senior Center

www.SeniorCenter@TownOfTivertonRI.com

207 Canonicus Street   Phone: (401) 625-6790

Tiverton, RI 02878   Fax: (401) 625-6793

Warren:

Warren Senior Center

www.Warren.RI.com

20 Libby Lane, Andreozzi Hall   Phone: (401) 247-1930

Warren, RI 02885   Fax: (401) 245-1392

Warwick:

JONAH Community Center

www.JonahCenterRI.com

830 Oakland Beach Avenue

Warwick, RI 02889

Phone: (401) 739-1305

Fax: (401) 732-3644

Pilgrim Senior Center

www.WarwickRI.gov

27 Pilgrim Parkway

Warwick, RI 02888

Phone: (401) 468-4090

Fax: (401) 468-4091

West Warwick:

West Warwick Senior Center

145 Washington Street

West Warwick, RI 02893

Phone: (401) 822-4450

Fax: (401) 828-2274

Westerly:

The Westerly Senior Citizens Center

www.WesterlySeniorCenter.org

39 State Street

Westerly, RI 02891

Phone: (401) 596-2404

Fax: (401) 596-4991

Woonsocket:

Woonsocket Senior Center

84 Social Street

Woonsocket, RI 02895

Phone: (401) 766-3734

Fax: (401) 765-5578

Notes

GERIATRIC CARE
MANAGEMENT

WHAT IS A GERIATRIC CARE MANAGER?

A Geriatric Care Manager (GCM) is a professional with specialized knowledge and expertise in senior care issues. Sometimes called case managers, elder care managers, service coordinators or care coordinators, GCMs are individuals who evaluate your situation, identify solutions, and work with you to design a plan for maximizing your elder's independence and well being.

Geriatric care management usually involves an in-depth assessment, developing a care plan, arranging for services, and following up or monitoring care. While you are not obligated to implement any part of the suggested care plan, Geriatric Care Managers often suggest potential alternatives you might not have considered, due to their experience and familiarity with community resources. They can also make sure your loved one receives the best possible care and any benefits to which they are entitled.

Geriatric Care Managers receive a variety of training, from bachelor degrees to multiple doctorates in gerontology, social work, psychology, and nursing. The following are just a few examples of types of credentials.

BSN—Bachelor of Science in Nursing

MPH—Master of Public Health

RN— Registered Nurse

MSW— Masters in Social Work

MHSA— Mental Health/Substance Abuse

LSW— Licensed Social Worker

CMC— Care Manager, Certified

Paula J. Foster, BSN, CMC, RN

Health Touch, Inc.

49 S County Commons Way

Wakefield, RI 02879

www.CNEHomeHealth.org

Phone: (401) 788-2400

Fax: (401) 788-9386

Paulette M. Masse, MHSA, LSW, CMC

Care Partnering

108 Beardsworth Road

Tiverton, RI 02878

www.CarePartnering.com

Phone: (401) 559-5668

Email: mpmasse1@cox.net

Francine Pare-Iarossi, RN

Specialty Personnel Services, Inc.

790 Charles Street

Providence, RI 02904

www.SpecialtyPersonnelServices.com

Phone: (401) 455-0111

Fax: (401) 455-0220

Jenny R. Miller, MSW

Senior Care Concepts Inc.

PO Box 2104

East Greenwich, RI 02818

www.SeniorCareConceptsInc.com

Phone: (401) 398-7655

Fax : (401) 739-4999

Carmen M. Roy, BSN, MPH, RN

Elder at Home, LLC

102 Slater Avenue

Providence, RI 02906

www.ElderAtHome.com

Phone: (401) 368-1088

Fax: (401) 453-1030

<u>Sage Senior Care Partners</u>

Care and Comfort Planning   *www.sagecarepartners.com*

959 North Main Street   Phone: (401) 437-6100

Providence, RI 02904

GERIATRIC ASSESSMENTS

GERIATRIC ASSESSMENTS

Geriatric assessment units conduct comprehensive assessments of a person's medical status. Seniors who have shown recent changes in their physical, psychological, or social functioning are candidates for assessment. A team of professionals identifies health and medical problems and plans a course of treatment. These organizations offer geriatric assessments:

OUTPATIENT GERIATRIC ASSESSMENTS

Butler Hospital Memory and Aging Program
Providence, RI

Phone: (401) 455-6403

www.MemoryDisorder.org

Founded in 1997, this program is dedicated to developing new treatments that improve the quality of life for patients and families dealing with memory loss. Affiliated with Brown Medical School, the program's mission is to assist individuals with memory loss, and their families, by providing comprehensive assessments and the latest treatments. The work of the Memory and Aging Program includes extensive research studies to develop new treatments for memory loss.

RI Mood and Memory Research Institute

East Providence, RI

Phone: (401) 435-8950

www.RIMMRI.com

Rhode Island Mood and Memory Research Institute welcomes generally healthy individuals living with a disease or condition looking to improve their quality of life. Clinical trials are open to all ages and each study has specific requirements. Study procedures, risks and benefits are explained by the study coordinator prior to participating in the study during the informed consent process.

Rhode Island and Miriam Hospitals Geriatrics

Practice & Services

Providence, RI

Phone: (401) 728-7270

Roger Williams Geriatric Consultation Service

North Providence, RI

Phone: (401) 231-0450

INPATIENT GERIATRIC ASSESSMENTS

Butler Hospital Senior Treatment Program

Providence, RI

Phone: (401) 455-6220

Butler Hospital's Senior treatment program offers a comprehensive approach to treating seniors who have depression, anxiety and memory disorders and patients who have cognitive disorders with complicating psychiatric behaviors. The Center's physicians are internationally recognized experts in caring for seniors with a dual diagnosis of a medical and a psychiatric illness and work alongside experienced nurses who are committed to working with older people affected by memory disorders and behavioral problems.

Roger Williams Medical Center Behavioral Health

Providence, RI

Phone: (401) 456-2363

Toll-Free: (800) 252-6466

Veterans Administration Mental Health

Providence, RI

Phone: (401) 457-3083

Notes

GERIATRIC PHYSICIANS

WHAT IS A GERIATRICIAN?

A Geriatrician is a medical doctor who specializes in the medical needs of seniors. All seniors should consult with a geriatrician for a geriatric assessment, even if they already have a family physician. A geriatric assessment is a comprehensive evaluation designed to optimize an older person's ability to enjoy good health, improve their overall quality of life, reduce the need for hospitalization or institutionalization and enable them to live independently for as long as possible.

David Dosa, M.D.

University Medical Foundation

407 East Avenue, Suite 110

Pawtucket, RI 02860

(401) 728-7270

David Fried, M.D.

Coastal Medical

1351 South County Trail

East Greenwich, RI

(401) 884-0333

Lynn McNicoll, M.D.

University Medical Foundation

407 East Avenue, Suite 110

Pawtucket, RI 02860

(401) 728-7270

John Murphy, M.D.

University Medical Foundation

407 East Avenue, Suite 110

Pawtucket, RI 02860

(401) 728-7270

Aman Nanda, M.D.

University Medical Foundation

407 East Avenue, Suite 110

Pawtucket, RI

(401) 728-7270

Syed R. Mehdi, M.D.

Landmark Primary Care

176 Cass Avenue

Woonsocket, RI 02895

(401) 765-3135

John Stoukides, M.D. (Geriatrician)

Roger Williams Senior Health Associates

2 Atlantic Boulevard

North Providence, RI 02911

(401) 231-0450

Notes

GERIATRIC NEUROLOGISTS

WHAT IS A GERIATRIC NEUROLOGIST?

As a Geriatric subspecialty, Geriatric Neurology focuses on neurological diseases and disorders that are common to older adults. The correct diagnosis of neurological disorders in older adults is difficult because signs of disease may mimic normal signs of aging. In addition, patients frequently have more than one neurological problem at a time. This subspecialty the result of growing recognition that neurological conditions may present differently in middle or late life, and that the older adult may require different treatments than younger patients.

One of the most common geriatric neurology problems is memory loss and dementia. In addition, many other neurological disorders are more common with age including, stroke, Parkinson's disease, seizures, and gait disorders. The subspecialty of geriatric neurology focuses on evaluating and treating these common neurological conditions in older adults.

NORTHERN RI

Dennis Aumentado, M.D.

RI Neurology Group, Inc.

1065 Mendon Road

Woonsocket, RI 02895

(401) 762-0170

Alla Korennaya, M.D.

175 Nate Whipple Highway, Suite 203

Cumberland, RI 02864

(401) 658-3600

GREATER PROVIDENCE

Motasem Al-Yacoub, M.D.

East Bay Neurology

333 School Street

Pawtucket, RI 02860

(401) 724-4100

Oscar Bernal, M.D.

University Medical Group

877 Chalkstone Avenue

Providence, RI 02908

(401) 456-2310

Joseph V. Centrofanti, M.D.

725 Reservoir Avenue, Suite 308

Cranston, RI 02910

(401) 944-9559

Guy Geffroy, M.D.

110 Lockwood Street

Providence, RI 02903

(401) 861-3040

Norman M. Gordon, M.D.

East Side Neurology

450 Veterans Memorial Parkway/ Building 11

East Providence, RI 02914

(401) 431-1860

Fred Griffith, M.D.

East Side Neurology

450 Veterans Memorial Parkway/ Building 11

East Providence, RI 02914

(401) 431-1860

Gary L'Europa, M.D.

Neurohealth, Inc.

227 Centerville Road

Warwick, RI 02886

(401) 732-3332

Albert J. Marano, M.D.

1526 Atwood Avenue, Suite 200

Johnston, RI 02919

(401) 272-7660

Thomas Morgan, M.D.

54 Jefferson Boulevard

Warwick, RI 02888

(401) 467-7720

Carlos H. Nieto, M.D.

300 Tollgate Road, Suite #301A

Warwick, RI 02886

(401) 739-4844

Brian R. Ott, M.D.

AD & Memory Disorders Center/ RI Hospital

Ambulatory Patient Center/ 6th Floor

593 Eddy Street

Providence, RI 02903

(401) 444-6440

Stephen Salloway, M. D.

Memory and Aging Program/Butler Hospital

345 Blackstone Boulevard

Providence, RI 02906

(401) 455-6403

Susan D. Weinman, M.D.

Long-term Care Psychiatry

345 Blackstone Boulevard/ Suite C-311

Providence, RI 02906

(401) 277-9935

Vlad Zayas, M.D.

East Side Neurology

450 Veterans Memorial Parkway/ Building 11

East Providence, RI 02914

(401) 431-1860

EAST BAY

Elaine C. Jones, M. D. (Neurologist)

Southern New England Neurology

1180 Hope Street (Bristol Medical Center)

Bristol, RI 02809

(401) 289-0992

Randy B. Kozel, M.D. (Neurologist)

Aquidneck Neurology

31 King Charles Drive

Portsmouth, RI 02871

(401) 683-9002

Brian R. Ott, M.D. (Neurologist)

Bristol Medical Center

1180 Hope Street

Bristol, RI 02809

(401) 253-8900

Suzanne Patrick-Mackinnon, M.D. (Neurologist)

Bristol Neurology Services

448 Hope Street/ Mezzanine Level

Bristol, RI 02809

(401) 254-6055

SOUTH COUNTY

Carlo Brogna, M.D. (Neurologist/Internal Medicine)

Coastal Neurology

101 Airport Road

Westerly, RI 02891

(401) 596-6207

Notes

ADULT
DAY CARE

WHAT IS ADULT DAY CARE?

Adult day care is a planned program of activities designed to promote well-being though social and health related services. Adult day care centers operate during daytime hours in a safe, supportive environment. Nutritious meals that accommodate special diets are typically included, along with an afternoon snack.

Adult day care centers can be public or private, non-profit or for-profit. The intent of an adult day center is primarily two-fold:

1) To provide older adults an opportunity to get out of the house and receive both mental and social stimulation

2) To give caregivers a much-needed break in which to attend to personal needs, or simply rest and relax.

Good candidates for adult day care are seniors who can benefit from the friendship and functional assistance a day care center offers or that may be physically or cognitively challenged but do not require 24-hour supervision.

Adult day care center participants need to be mobile, with the possible assistance of a cane, walker or wheelchair, and in most cases, they must also be continent.

Common recreational activities include arts and crafts, musical entertainment, mental stimulation games, exercise, discussion groups, holiday and birthday celebrations, local outings, and intergenerational programs.

Besides recreational activities, some adult day care centers provide transportation to and from the center, social services including counseling and support groups for caregivers, and health support services such as blood pressure monitoring and vision screening. Often, adult day care centers provide health assessments and therapy if staffed with a Registered Nurse or other health professionals. Other types of adult day care provide social and health services specifically for individuals with Alzheimer's Disease (including early-onset) or other memory/dementia related disorders.

The cost for an adult day care center ranges but is typically set on a per day basis. Many facilities offer services on a sliding fee scale, meaning that what you pay is based on your income and ability to pay. Be sure to ask about financial assistance.

Cornerstone Adult Services, Inc., Bristol Center

172 Franklin Street

Bristol, RI 02809

Phone: (401) 254-9629

Fax: (401) 254-1597

www.Cornerstone-RI.com

Contact: Carly Ellison

Social Worker

Hours of Operation:

Monday-Friday 7:30am-4:30pm

Founded in 1973, Cornerstone Adult Services, Inc., is a not-for-profit community based organization that helps frail elderly and adults with disabilities remain at home and in their communities. They provide a planned program of health, social and support services in a protective day setting. Each participant has a personalized plan of services to maximize cognitive and physical abilities.

Participants: 15-20

The Willows Adult Day Care

47 Barker Avenue

Warren, RI 02885

Phone: (401) 245-2323

Fax: (401) 247-9030

www.RhodeIandNursing.net

Contact: Paula Lage

Director

Hours of Operation:

Monday-Friday 7:30am-4:30pm

Saturday 8:00am-4pm

Since 1966, The Willows Adult Day Center has been serving those living in the East Bay. Their adult day services provide an interactive program of medical, social, and therapeutic services to those individuals who are either physically or cognitively challenged. Their comprehensive services, coupled with member-specific care plans, assure the highest level of wellness and functioning for loved ones and can provide members with the respite and peace of mind that one may require.

Participants: 30-35

Cornerstone Adult Services, Inc., Alzheimer's Center

140 Warwick Neck Avenue

Warwick, RI 02889

Phone: (401) 739-2844

Fax: (401) 739-5388

www.Cornerstone-RI.com

Contact: Dottie Santagata, Director

Carly Ellison, Social Worker

Hours of Operation:

Monday-Friday 7:30am-6:00pm

Saturday 9:00am-5:00pm

Founded in 1973, Cornerstone Adult Services, Inc., is a not-for-profit community based organization that helps frail elderly and adults with disabilities remain at home and in their communities. The center in Warwick is one of the only two Alzheimer's specific day care centers in the state. The services are not just for Alzheimer's Disease, but also for other dementia type illnesses. They provide a planned program of health, social and support services in a protective day setting. Each participant has a personalized plan of services to maximize cognitive and physical abilities. Skilled Nursing services are available.

Participants: 30-40

Cornerstone Adult Services, Inc., Apponaug Center

3720 Post Road

Warwick, RI 02886

Phone: (401) 739-2847

www.Cornerstone-RI.com

Contact: Carly Ellison

Social Worker

Hours of Operation:

Monday-Friday 7:30am-4:30pm

Founded in 1973, Cornerstone Adult Services, Inc., is a not-for-profit community based organization that helps frail elderly and adults with disabilities remain at home and in their communities. They provide a planned program of health, social and support services in a protective day setting. Each participant has a personalized plan of services to maximize cognitive and physical abilities. Skilled Nursing services are available.

Participants: 30-35

Cornerstone Adult Services, Inc., Coventry Center

60 Wood Street

Coventry, RI 02816

Phone: (401) 822-6212

www.Cornerstone-RI.com

Contact: Carly Ellison

Social Worker

Hours of Operation:

Monday-Friday 7:30-4:30pm

Founded in 1973, Cornerstone Adult Services, Inc., is a not-for-profit community based organization that helps frail elderly and adults with disabilities remain at home and in their communities. They provide a planned program of health, social and support services in a protective day setting. Each participant has a personalized plan of services to maximize cognitive and physical abilities. Skilled Nursing services are available.

Participants: 15-25

Forest Farm Adult Day Services

193 Forest Avenue

Middletown, RI 02842

Phone: (401) 849-8326

Fax: (401) 848-7403

www.ForestFarmHealthcare.com

Contact: Rita St. Laurent, RN

Adult Day Care Director

Hours of Operation:

Monday-Friday 8:00am-4:00pm

Forest Farm Health Care Centre has been providing services to the Aquidneck Island community since 1983. Forest Farm Adult Day Services offers two unique program levels. One program level is designed for alert but mildly forgetful seniors who would benefit from social interaction with their peers. The second program level is designed for the more physically frail or those who need more assistance.

Participants: 15-25

Nancy Brayton Osborn Adult Day Health Center

115 East Main Road

Little Compton, RI 02837

Phone: (401) 635-2358

Fax: (401) 635-1694

Contact: Kathryn Cullen

Adult Day Care Director

Hours of Operation:

Monday-Friday 8:30am-2:30pm

The Nancy Brayton Osborn Center offers programs to help adults who have Alzheimer's Disease as well as those with a functional, emotional and/or developmental disability. The center offers recreational and social activities, assistance with activities of daily living, medication assessment and monitoring, respite time and caregiver support services.

Participants: 15-20

Alternative Adult Care

84 Social Street	Contact: Joanne Mondor
Woonsocket, RI 02895	Director
Phone:(401) 766-0516	Hours of Operation:
Fax: (401) 765-5578	Monday-Friday 7:30am-3:00pm

www.SeniorServicesri.org/AAC.htm

Alternative Adult Care offers a variety of social services, daily exercise and meals, activities, outings and current event discussions. Counseling and referral services are available. Financial assistance is available to those who are eligible. A registered nurse is in attendance daily.

Participants: 25-30

Comprehensive Adult Day Center

100 Niantic Avenue	Contact: Jennifer Minuto
Providence, RI 02907	Director
Phone: (401) 351-2440	Hours of Operation:
Fax: (401) 421-5905	Monday-Friday 7:30am-4:30pm

www.JSARI.org/DayCare

The Jewish Seniors Agency Comprehensive Adult Day Center is licensed by the Department of Elderly Affairs and is open to both Jewish and non -Jewish members of the community. With the belief that the key to health and happiness lies in the continued stimulation of the mind and spirit, their all-inclusive program offers therapy for both. Participants enjoy daily recreational and social therapy and the center also offers a Wellness Program. As the only Kosher Adult Day Center in the state, they serve two meals each day. The center, designed as a nurturing environment for seniors with physical impairments, dementia and those suffering from the early stages of Alzheimer's, places emphasis on interacting socially with others. They provide an on-staff registered nurse, case manager, and certified nursing assistants which help to ensure that the medical needs of participants are also addressed.

Cranston Adult Day Services

1070 Cranston Street

Cranston, RI 02920

Phone: (401) 780-6243

Fax: (401) 946-5909

rcastiglione@cransonri.com

Contact: Rosalind M. Castiglione, RN

Director

Hours of Operation:

Monday-Friday 7:45am-5:00pm

Cranston Adult Day Services is a division of the Cranston Department of Senior Services and is licensed by the Department of Elderly Affairs. It is a comprehensive program designed to meet the medical, social, and psychological needs of the frail and/or disabled population. They offer a vast assortment of services including therapeutic programs, recreational activities, medical monitoring, meals and arranging for transportation. Fees are based on a sliding scale. Assistance with application for State sponsored financial support is available.

Dora C. Howard Centre, Ltd.

715 Putnam Pike

Greenville, RI 02828

Phone: (401) 949-3890

Fax: (401) 949-5666

www.DoraCHoward.com

Contact: Lori Kirkwood

Director

Hours of Operation:

Monday-Friday 7:30am-5:00pm

Established in 1985, Dora C. Howard is a non-profit organization licensed by the Department of Elderly Affairs. Day services are offered to elder residents of Burrillville, Foster, Glocester, Johnston, Lincoln, North Smithfield, Scituate and Smithfield. The center provides a catered program with RN supervision, case management, health monitoring, individualized plans of care, nutritional meals, structured activities and socialization, unisex salon services and podiatry services.

Fruit Hill Day Services for Elderly

399 Fruit Hill Avenue

North Providence, RI 02911

Phone: (401) 353-5805

Fax: (401) 353-4904

Contact: Sr. Aline Giroux

Executive Director

Hours of Operation:

Monday-Friday 8:00am-4:00pm

Fruit Hill Day Services, established in 1973, is a non-profit organization operated by the Franciscan Missionaries of Mary and licensed by the Department of Elderly Affairs. Services provided include but are not limited to case management, nursing care, nutritious meals and a program of activities organized to accommodate various levels of functioning. A limited amount of transportation is provided. The program seeks to enhance participants quality of life and to minimize or retard the need for institutionalized care.

Generations Adult Health Center

1073 Mineral Spring Avenue

North Providence, RI 02904

Phone: (401) 725-6400

Fax: (401) 722-5916

www.GenerationsPrograms.com

Contact: Gregory Andrade

Executive Director

Hours of Operation:

Monday-Friday 7:00am-5:00pm

Saturday: 8:30am-1:30pm

Sunday: 10:00am-3:00pm

Since 1999, The Generations Program has been providing an all-day setting designed to maximize abilities in daily functioning while supporting the dignity of participants and promoting personal independence. Generations Adult Day Health Center provides participants with two full meals daily. Programs are specifically designed to meet different age and ability levels (21+) and include but are not limited to exercise, education, horticulture, pet therapy, culinary programs, music and dancing, religious and intergenerational activities. A registered nurse is available to administer medication. Generations is the only adult day care facility that specializes in brain injury in Rhode Island.

Hope Alzheimer's Center

25 Brayton Avenue

Cranston, RI 02920

Phone: (401) 946-9220

Fax: (401) 946-3850

www.HopeAlzheimersCenter.org

Contact: Cynthia Conant-Arp

Executive Director

Hours of Operation:

Monday-Friday   7:45am-5:00pm

Saturday   9:00am-4:00pm

Hope Alzheimer's Center is a nationally recognized facility with a single goal—making life better, fuller and more secure for people with Alzheimer's disease and other memory disorders since 1995. The center is one of the only two Alzheimer's specific day care centers in the state. Program activities include exercise, art and music programs, movement therapy, a men's club and intergenerational programs. Personal care and skilled nursing is available. Care is available on site and includes medication management, glucose monitoring, injections, podiatry services, therapy and routine health assessments. The center also offers social services, care management, hair care, podiatry and transportation assistance.

An average of 50 participants are served daily.

New Horizons Adult Day Center

426 Main Street

Pawtucket, RI 02860

Phone: (401)727-0950

www.newhorizonsadc.org

Contact: Melissa A. Smith,

Director

Hours of Operation:

Monday-Friday 7:30-5:00pm

New Horizons follows a medical model and offers a multitude of assistive services to its program participants, including nursing ,case management, therapeutic recreation, and dialing living services. We recommend that all new participants attend a minimum of two days per week to establish a sense of routine and to form social connections. The cost of the program is to be determined upon admission and we ask that you please provide a copy of current insurance information and your Social Security Card. We all require that all new participants have physician orders completed prior to starting the program.

New Horizons supports a diverse group of individuals with varying diagnoses including but not limited to Parkinson's disease, Multiple Sclerosis, Alzheimer's disease, Dementia, Diabetes, Depression, and other chronic illnesses.

New Horizons Adult Day Care is a private, non-profit adult day program licensed by the Rhode Island Department of Health. We are committed to providing the highest quality of adult day services to frail elders and functionally impaired adults in a safe, therapeutic environment, while also providing respite for caregiver and education for the community.

We would like to extend an invitation for you to visit our program and witness first hand how critical our adult day center service is to the participants and caregivers we assist daily. Please drop in for a tour or contact the Director, Melissa a. Smith, to schedule a meeting to learn more about our program.

South Kingstown Adult Day Services

283 Post Road

Wakefield, RI 02879

Phone: (401) 783-8736

Fax: (401) 792-9609

Contact: Rick Ryan

Senior Services Director

Hours of Operation:

Monday-Friday 8:30am-3:30pm

www.southkingstownri.com/code/snrsvc_daycare.cfm

Operated by the town of South Kingstown, The Adult Day Services Center provides an array of supportive services designed to increase the activities of daily living for older persons dependent upon continual family support and supervision. The program provides supervised supportive care for frail elderly persons to meet the needs of the functionally impaired individual. The program also provides respite and emotional support to caregivers.

Participants: 20

Westerly Adult Day Services

65 Wells Street

Westerly, RI 02891

Phone: (401) 596-1336

Fax: (401) 596-6186

Contact: Karen Hawthorn

Social Worker

Hours of Operation:

Monday-Friday: 7:30am-4:00pm

www.WADSInc.com

Westerly Adult Day Services offers a variety of social services to keep participants engaged and stimulated. The Center offers nursing supervision, health monitoring, respite care and family consultation, nutritious meals and therapeutic recreation.

Participants: 25-30

LIVE AND LEARN
PROGRAMS

The Live and Learn Program is designed specifically for persons who have been diagnosed with ***early memory loss***. The program provides a social support system outside of the family. It helps to increase self-esteem, avoid isolation, and improves mental and physical fitness in a safe and secure environment. Sessions are held as follows:

Tuesdays from 9:30-11:30am at the Warwick Public Library;

Tuesdays from 12:30-2:00pm at Providence– Bliss Properties;

Tuesdays from 10:00-1200pm at Middletown St Lucy's Church;

Wednesdays from 9:30-11:30am at the Woonsocket Public Library;

Thursdays from 10:30-12:00pm at North Kingstown St. Francis de Sales Parish;

An interview with a staff person is required to determine whether the program meets the applicant's needs.

For further information about the Live and Learn Program please contact the Alzheimer's Association—Rhode Island Chapter at **(401) 421-0008** or visit them online at *www.alz.org/ri*

The Live & Learn Program is funded through a grant from the Department of Elderly Affairs.

alzheimer's ᏛᏜ association

State of Rhode Island
Department of Elderly Affairs

Notes

HOME HEALTH CARE

WHAT IS HOME HEALTH CARE?

Home care typically refers to medical and/or non-medical services that assist individuals with activities of daily living.

Home care is becoming an increasingly popular choice for care because it enables individuals to remain in their own environments longer and helps families better plan for the future care of a loved one.

Many families utilize home care agencies to supplement the services they cannot perform themselves for a loved one due to work and other family commitments. These agencies provide an extra pair of hands and assist in the overall care management of a loved one.

Most agencies can provide services for as little as six hours a week up to 24 hours a day, seven days a week. The schedules are usually determined during the assessment process and vary depending on the needs of both the family caregiver and the needs of the client.

Caregivers need to be reminded that they are at health risk if they try to take on too much and forget to take care of themselves. It is just as important that the caregiver is getting proper nutrition, rest, and exercise as it is for the person they are caring for.

THE FACTS ABOUT HOME CARE

- Falls are the leading cause of home injury.

- People aged 75 years and older who fall are four to fives times more likely to be admitted to a LTC facility for a year or longer.

- Nearly 25% of American adults provide assistance to a parent or relative.

- One in four caregivers say the person they care for lives with them.

DIFFICULTIES CAREGIVERS EXPERIENCE:

- Burnout

- Stress

- Other family / job responsibilities

- Struggle to balance tasks

- Health problems

WHO MAY NEED NON-MEDICAL HOME CARE?

- Seniors who are living at home and having difficulty performing their *IADLs*. (*Instrumental Activities of Daily Living*)

WHAT ARE INSTRUMENTAL ACTIVITIES OF DAILY LIVING (IADLs)?

- Using the telephone
- Grocery Shopping
- Preparing Meals
- Managing Money
- Doing Laundry
- Opening Mail
- Getting to places beyond walking distance
- Taking Medications
- Doing Housework

WHAT ARE ACTIVITIES OF DAILY LIVING (ADLs)

- Bathing Assistance
- Dressing
- Feeding
- Transferring (non-ambulatory)
- Toileting
- Nail Clipping
- Brushing Hair
- Administering Medications

MEDICAL VS. NON-MEDICAL HOME CARE AGENCIES

NON-MEDICAL AGENCIES	MEDICAL AGENCIES
Provides Caregiver assistance to those who are having difficulty performing their IDALs	Provides nursing care to those who cannot perform their ADLs
Provides Companionship and Homemaker services ensuring a safe setting	Personal care specialists who provide or assist with personal care, ambulating, incontinence management, and feeding
In-house safety assessments	In-house safety assessments
Prompting and cueing for ADLs	Brushing hair, toileting, feeding, hands on assist in doing personal hygiene
Medication Reminders	Administer Medications
Stand-by assistance for bathing	Bathing – hands on
Meal preparation, light housekeeping, laundry, transportation, companionship, sitting services	Will usually refer out to a non-medical home care agency that provides housekeeping, companionship, and sitting services

WHAT ARE SOME IMPORTANT QUESTIONS TO ASK WHEN MAKING A DECISION ON AN AGENCY?

NON-MEDICAL AGENCIES	MEDICAL AGENCIES
What services are performed?	What services are performed?
Are the caregivers bonded and insured?	Are the certified nursing assistants bonded and insured?
Are your caregivers trained and supervised?	Does your staff work under the supervision of a Registered Nurse?
What are your backup procedures for a no show?	What are your backup procedures for a no show?
How is communication with the family maintained?	How is communication with the family maintained?
Do you have a 24-hour on call supervisor?	Do you have a 24-hour on call supervisor?

FUNDING FOR MEDICAL VS. NON-MEDICAL HOME CARE

NON-MEDICAL HOME CARE	MEDICAL HOME CARE
Private Pay	Private Pay
Long Term Care Insurance	Most Insurance's including long term care insurance
State funding if eligible	Medicare/Medicaid

—WHAT TO ASK—

The following are some questions you should ask when choosing a home care agency:

- **Is the agency licensed by the R. I. Department of Health?**

  State licensed agencies are required to meet rigorous quality standards such as background checks, educational requirements and employee health screenings. For this reason, only licensed agencies are certified to provide hands-on care for your loved one. While many companies may *propose* that they follow strict guidelines, licensed agencies must *comply*, and they are routinely surveyed for compliance.

- **Does the agency offer health services or strictly companion care?**

  Sometime you can use two different agencies, depending on your needs.

- **Is there a high turnover of employees within the agency?**

  It is difficult for a senior or disabled individual when home care involves meeting new caregivers on a regular basis. Most seniors and disabled individuals favor routine and consistency.

- **How long has the Agency been in business?**

  This isn't always dispositive, but as a rule, with longevity comes stability and expertise.

- **When you call the agency, how are you received?**

  Can you talk with a live person, or are you requested to leave a call back number? Is the person handling your call concerned and knowledgeable? Responsiveness is very important when you are dealing with issues involving health and family. This is particularly true if the family is not local and relies heavily on the agency to provide care to their loved one.

DEPARTMENT OF ELDERLY AFFAIRS CO-PAY PROGRAM

AND

CASE MANAGEMENT AGENCIES

DEPARTMENT OF ELDERLY AFFAIRS

HOME AND COMMUNITY CARE

CO-PAYMENT PROGRAM

For persons who meet the guidelines for the Department of Elderly Affairs Care Co-Payment Program, services are offered at a reduced rate to Rhode Island residents aged 65 and over and homebound. There are also annual income guidelines for single and married persons that will determine eligibility in the program. Currently the annual income limits are $19,785 for a single person, and $24,735 for a married person. These guidelines change annually. Once eligible, the participants will pay a co-pay, which is determined by the participant's income.

Based on eligibility, these services may include home health aide services, adult day services, personal emergency response systems, meals, transportation, senior companions, minor home modifications, and minor assistive devices.

The Department of Elderly Affairs works with a network of regional Case Management Agencies to develop care plans and to determine eligibility for programs. A case manager will be assigned to perform an assessment and coordinate services for the participant. These plans help seniors remain in their homes with a maximum independence.

Call the Agency that services your community for more information, or call the Department of Elderly Affairs at 401-462-0570, www.dea.state.ri.us.

The following are a list of Case Management Agencies:

Casework Referral Advocacy (CRA)

*www.*nricommunityservices.org

60 Wood Street   Phone: (401822-6240

Coventry, RI 02816

Communities served: Block Island, Coventry, Exeter, Jamestown, North Kingstown, South County, and Washington County

Child and Family of Newport County– Elder Care

*www.*cfsnewport.org

31 John Clark Road   Phone: (401) 845-2270

Middletown, RI 02842

Communities served: Aquidneck Island, Newport County

East Bay Community Action Program

*www.*ebcap.org

100 Bullocks Point Avenue   Phone: (401) 437-5102

Riverside, RI 02915

Communities served: Bristol, Central Falls, East Bay, and Pawtucket

Meals on Wheels of Rhode Island

70 Bath Street   Phone: (401) 351-6700

Providence, RI 02908

Communities Served: Providence

Tri-Town Community Action Program

*www.*tri-town.org

1126 Hartford Avenue   Phone: (401) 351-2750

Johnston, RI 02919   (401) 349-5760

Communities served: Burillville, Chepachet, Cumberland,
Cranston, Foster, Glocester, Johnston, Lincoln, North Providence,
North Smithfield, Scituate, Smithfield, Westerly, and Woonsocket

West Bay Community Action Program

*www.*westbaycap.org

208 Buttonwoods Avenue   Phone: (401) 732-4660

Warwick, RI 02886   extension 130

Communities served: Coventry, East Greenwich, Warwick, and West Warwick

HOME CARE &
COMMUNITY CARE
AGENCIES

Bayside Nursing, LLC   www.BaysideNursing.com

177 Airport Road   Phone: (401) 921-5995

Warwick, RI 02889   Fax: (401) 921-5998

The concept of Bayside Nursing, LLC was conceived in 2002. Bayside Nursing offers both skilled and non-skilled services for both short and long term care. Care can be directly coordinated with existing physicians. Services include but are not limited to: preparation of meals, grooming, bathing, light-housekeeping, companionship, transportation, errands, and prescription and case management coordination.

Medical

Homefront Health Care   www.Homefront.org

335 East Centerville Road   Phone: (401) 738-0409

Warwick, RI 02886   Fax: (401) 738-0597

Since 1966 Homefront Health Care, a non-profit organization, has been serving Rhode Island families. Homefront is licensed by the Rhode Island Department of Health, accredited by the Joint Commission on Accreditation of Healthcare Organizations and a participating member of CareLink and United Way. Both skilled and non-skilled services can be provided. Services include but are not limited to: respite care, adult nursing, advocate service, medication management, home repair, emergency response, personal care and socialization. All services are available, on a limited basis, at a reduced rate for anyone unable to afford the full cost of care.

Medicaid accepted

Medical

Coventry Home Care, Inc.

1060 Tioque Avenue   Phone: (401) 823-5300

Coventry, Rhode Island 02816   Fax: (401) 823-0897

Medicaid accepted

| Medical |

Odyssey Healthcare of Rhode Island

1-877-637-9432   www.odsyhealth.com

2374 Post Road, Suite 206   Phone: (401) 738-1492

Warwick, RI 02886   Fax: (401) 738-4029

VNA of Rhode Island

475 Kilvert Street   www.vnari.org

Warwick, RI 02886   Phone: (401) 574-4900

                                       Toll Free: 1-800-638-6274

Referrals may contact intake department directly at 401-574-4950 or fax information to 401-490-8870.

The POINT

171 Service Road   www.thepointri.org

Warwick, RI 02886   Phone: (401) 462-4444

The Point can provide information regarding non-profit and private home care agencies in Rhode Island. Hours of operation are Monday, Wednesday, and Friday 8:30am-4:00pm.

Right at Home   *www.Providence.RightAtHome.net*

1345 Jefferson Boulevard, Suite 1W   Phone: (401) 384-6485

Warwick, RI 02886   Fax: (401) 384-6487

Right at Home is a national franchise organization offering in-home care and assistance. Right at Home does not provide skilled nursing services. Services provide by caregivers include but are not limited to: socialization, indoor/outdoor activities, personal care, Alzheimer's and dementia care, homemaker services, transportation, and light housekeeping.

| Medical |

Senior Helpers   *www.SeniorHelpers.com*

60 Quaker Lane   Phone: (401) 825-7200

Warwick, RI 02886   Fax: (401) 825-7204

Senior Helpers is a licensed Home Care Provider agency specializing in personal and companion in-home care. Senior Helpers does not provide skilled nursing services. Services provided include but are not limited to: companionship, personal care, Alzheimer's and dementia care, light housekeeping, transportation and medication reminders,

---

VNA of Care New England   *www.CNEHomeHealth.org*

51 Health Lane   Phone: (401) 737-6050

Warwick, RI 02886   Fax: (401) 738-0247

VNA of Care New England is a non-profit home health care agency accredited by the Joint Commission. VNA of Care New England provides skilled nursing, physical, occupational, and speech therapy and hospice services to people throughout Rhode Island. Specialty services include wound care, cardiac rehabilitations, diabetic care and falls prevention. VNA of Care New England accepts almost all payers.

| Medical |

Visiting Nurse Services of Newport & Bristol Counties

1184 East Main Road   *www.VNSRI.com*

P.O. Box 690   Phone: (401) 682-2100

Portsmouth, RI 02871   Fax: (401) 682-2111

Visiting Nurse Services of Newport & Bristol Counties is a not-for-profit agency providing home care, hospice, community health education and clinics. VNS is a provider of registered nurses, physical, occupational and speech therapies, registered dieticians, social work, home health aides and homemaker care. VNS is a vendor for Philips Lifeline personal response systems. Medicare, Medicaid pay and sliding scale fees are accepted. No one is refused for inability to pay.

Medical

Visiting Nursing Service of Southeastern Massachusetts

Little Compton Office

115 East Main Road   www.vnasm.org

Little Compton, RI 02837   Phone: (401)635-2358

Medical

Bayada Nurses   *www.Bayada.com*

2 Charles Street   Phone: (401) 273-1112

Providence, RI 02904   Fax: (401) 273-5705

Bayada Nurses has been dedicated to national home care since their foundation in 1975. They offer a wide range of services to meet the needs of their clients. Both private duty nursing services and skilled intermittent care services are available. Services include but are not limited to: skilled nursing, personal care, homemaking, therapy and rehabilitation.

| Medical |

CarePoint Partners   *www.carepointpartners.com*

15 Hazel Street   Phone: (401) 727-6100

Pawtucket, RI 02860   Fax: (401) 727-6120

Founded in Rhode Island, Clinical I.V. Network is a recognized leader in providing home infusion therapies as a cost-effective alternative to hospitalization. The Network is accredited by the Joint Commission on Accreditation of Healthcare Organizations. Clinical I.V. Network offers an array of infusion related therapies including but not limited to: antibiotic therapies, chemotherapy, pain management, hydration and pre/post transplant care.

| Medical |

Cathleen Naughton Associates
www.cathleennaughtonassoc.com

249 Wickenden Street   Phone: (401) 751-9660

Providence, RI 02903   Fax: (401) 831-2157

| Medical |

Jewish Family Service   *www.jfsri.org*

959 North Main Street   Phone: (401) 331-1244

Providence, RI 02904

Jewish Family Service of Rhode Island provides trained and licensed Certified Nursing Assistants to assist the sick, the elderly, and the temporarily disabled at home. The goal is to enable these individuals to maintain their independence. Help is provided for personal care and meal prepa-

---

PARI   *www.pari-ilc.org*

500 Prospect Street   Phone: (401) 725-1966

Pawtucket, RI 02860

PARI provides information regarding services, housing, or transportation related to home and community care. PARI also runs a personal care assistant program called Personal Choice.

Volunteer Nursing Organizations

23 Dellwood Avenue   Phone: (401) 946-2117

Cranston, RI 02920

The Volunteer Nursing Organization provides in home nursing care services at no cost. Call the program for more information.

Visiting Nurse Service of Greater RI

6 Blackstone Place   Phone: (401) 769-5670

Lincoln, RI 02865   www.vnsgri.org

PACE Organization of Rhode Island

225 Chapman Street

Providence, RI 02905

Phone: (401) 490-6566

Fax: (401) 490-6537

www.PACE-RI.org

Hours of Operation: Monday-Friday 7:30am-5:00pm

The PACE (Program of All-Inclusive Care for the Elderly) program co-ordinates and provides all needed preventive, primary, acute and long term care services so that older individuals can continue living in the community.

In order to join the PACE Program a participant must:

- Be at least 55 years or older

- Live in Rhode Island (excluding Block Island and Prudence Island)

- Be able to meet the nursing home level of care requirements of the Rhode Island Department of Human Services

- Be able to live in the community without jeopardizing one's health or safety

Comprehensive care that meets the participant's needs includes: personalized primary care in the PACE Center by physicians and nurses trained to care for older people, access by appointment to medical specialists such as dentists, optometrists, audiologists, podiatrists and psychiatrists, prescription drugs and medical equipment, in-home services, transportation to and from the PACE Center, Medical equip-ment, physical, Speech and Occupational therapies to help participants function better day-to-day, and therapeutic activities at the PACE Center.

If you have Medicaid or are eligible for both Medicare and Medicaid, you may receive care from the PACE Organization of Rhode Island at no cost. Call PACE for more information regarding the program and the eligibility requirements.

Home Care Services   www.jfsri.org

(formerly Jewish Family Service Homecare)

959 North Main Street   Phone: (401) 331-6962

Providence, RI 02904   Fax: (410) 331-5772

The mission of the Jewish Family service is to sustain, nurture and strengthen the emotional and general well-being and stability of families and individuals throughout the life cycle.

Phenix Home Care, Inc.

227 Phenix Avenue   Phone: (401) 943-6230

Cranston, RI 02920   Fax: (401) 943-6265

Medical
Medicaid Accepted

Maxim Healthcare Services   www.maximhealthcare.com

758 Eddy Street   Phone: (401) 751-6333

Providence, RI 02901   Fax: (401) 751-6338

A full service healthcare company with a reputation for providing innovative solutions that improve health and enhance the quality of life for patients. Dedicated to customer services and improving patient care and committed to staffing quality healthcare professionals.

Medical

HealthTouch

www.CNEHomeHealth.org

49 South County Commons Way

Phone: (401) 788-2400

Wakefield, RI 02879

Fax: (401) 788-9386

HealthTouch is a non-profit private pay home nursing agency accredited by the Joint Commission and licensed by the State of Rhode Island to provide medical and non-medical care to people of all ages. Services include assistance with bathing and grooming, companion care, medication management, shopping, and/or errands, transportation to doctor's appointments, Lifeline Personal Emergency Response system, and Geriatric Care Management. HealthTouch staff are comprised of registered nurses and certified nursing assistants, all licensed by the Rhode Island Department of Health.

| Medical |

Home Instead Senior Care

www.HomeInstead.com

7291 Post Road

Phone: (401) 667-2923

North Kingstown, RI 02852

Fax: (401) 667-2928

VNS Home Health Services

14 Woodruff Avenue, Suite 7

Phone: 1-800-739-2920

Narragansett, RI 02879

www.vnshomehealth.org

Notes

LEGAL PLANNING

WHO NEEDS TO CONSIDER LONG-TERM CARE PLANNING?

The four primary sources for funding long-term care costs are private pay, long-term care insurance, Medicare, and Medicaid. Medicare is very limited, and most senior clients do not have, or cannot afford, long-term care insurance. With that said, almost everyone who needs an institutional level of care eventually relies on Medicaid for payment. This is true because the costs are catastrophic and there are very few people who can afford to private pay for an extended period of time, particularly without impoverishing a healthy spouse who may be living in the community.

Financial planners, accountants, those in the health field, as well as prospective clients, often ask us "when should someone think about long-term care planning?" Many people mistakenly believe that long-term care planning is completely financially driven. The truth is that anyone over the age of sixty, or handicapped, or with a progressive disease or other health issue, should be engaging in long -term care planning. Any senior who owns a home should consider planning. Married couples should be particularly careful to engage in advanced long-term care planning, so as not to impoverish the healthier spouse should long-term care be needed. Even younger people should engage in long-term care planning through the use of a proper long-term care insurance policy.

Finally, it is crucial to seek the advice of an attorney experienced in elder law and estate planning. All too often, clients come into our office and tell us, "I know I did something with the deed ... but I don't know what." If this is the case in your situation, or for a client you know, the documents and transactions should be reviewed immediately.

Additionally, if transfers have been made in the past it is very important that enough funds were reserved to pay through any period of ineligibility for Medicaid, as a result of the transfer. It is never too late to do planning, however the options available, as well as the savings to the client, will be severely limited if the individual waits until crisis strikes.

By Laura M. Krohn, Attorney at Law, Author

Senior Resource Guide of Rhode Island

To schedule an appointment with Laura please call:

401-398-8383

Laura M. Krohn Elder Law Attorney

Senior Resource Clinic

631 Main Street

East Greenwich, Rhode Island 02818

www.seniorguideri.com

MEDICARE BASICS

Medicare is a federal health insurance program that provides benefits to the elderly and the disabled. Medicare is an entitlement and is available to individuals who are age 65 or over, the disabled, and those with permanent kidney failure.

Individuals with disabilities who are eligible for Social Security Disability Income (SSDI) and receive SSDI for a 24 month period will also qualify for Medicare.

Individuals with end-stage renal disease qualify for Medicare three months after beginning renal dialysis.

Basically, Rhode Island Seniors who have Medicare have one of three parts: Part A, Part B, and Part D, which are described as follows:

Medicare Part A:

Part A provides coverage for hospitalization, home health care, skilled nursing facility care, and hospice care. Part A coverage is offered at no charge to persons age 65 and older who are entitled to receive Social Security and Railroad Retirement benefits. Those age 65 and older not entitled to receive Social Security may "buy-in" to Medicare by paying a premium. Disabled individuals eligible for Medicare receive Part A benefits free of charge.

Medicare Part B:

Part B provides coverage for physician's services, diagnostic test, medical equipment, ambulance services, certain home care, and physical and speech therapy. Unlike Part A benefits, Part B requires the payment of a premium for all beneficiaries. Usually, this is automatically deducted from an individual's monthly Social Security income check.

Medicare Part D:

Part D provides beneficiaries with assistance with paying for prescription drugs. Part D coverage is not provided within the traditional Medicare program. Beneficiaries must enroll in one of many Part D plans offered by private companies.

For more information on Medicare health coverage, contact The Centers for Medicare and Medicaid Services (CMS) at www.cms.gov or call 1-800-MEDICARE. The mission of the CMS is to ensure effective, up-to-date health coverage.

By Laura M. Krohn, Attorney at Law, Author

Senior Resource Guide of Rhode Island

To schedule an appointment with Laura please call:

401-398-8383

Laura M. Krohn Elder Law Attorney

Senior Resource Clinic

631 Main Street

East Greenwich, Rhode Island 02818

www.seniorguideri.com

MEDICAID BASICS

There are many different Medicaid Programs in Rhode Island that apply to seniors. There are programs that pay for care at home, in assisted living residences, in nursing homes, and adult day care centers.

Medicaid is different than Medicare because Medicare is an entitlement. Also, Medicare does not pay for custodial care in a nursing home; Medicare pays for a short period while a patient is rehabilitating (See the Medicare section for more information).

Rhode Island Institutional Medicaid rules will require that individuals meet the following tests, in addition to other state specific requirements:

1. **Citizenship:** An applicant for Institutional Medicaid must be a United States Citizen or a "qualified alien" (a permanent resident, an asylee, a refugee, a person paroled into the United States for at least a year, or a person granted conditional entry).

2. **Residence:** An Applicant must be a resident of the state where the application is being made.

3. **Medical Need**: The state will perform a medical evaluation of the applicant to qualify the applicant as needing long-term care.

4. **Resource Requirements**: Rhode Island requires that an applicant have available resources worth less than $4,000. The spouses of married applicants are also limited as to what resources they may keep.

5. **Income Requirements:** States vary, but in Rhode Island Income eligibility is met by the inability to the pay the actual cost of private care with available income.

Prior to applying for Medicaid, it is very important that the applicant and/or her family seek advice as to eligibility. Uniformed and misinformed applicants often apply for benefits and are denied for various reason, the following being the most popular reasons:

1. Resource requirements have not been met.

2. Assets were given away in order to qualify for Medicaid and the application was made during a period of ineligibility.

The spouse of a married applicant must be proactive in getting correct legal advice from an elder law attorney familiar with Rhode Island law, so as to not become impoverished by the institutionalized spouse's long-term care costs.

Not all nursing homes participate in the Medicaid program. Therefore, it is crucial that families ask the facility of choice whether or not they do participate in Medicaid. If the facility does not participate in the Medicaid program, the resident will need to be relocated once his/her private funds are exhausted.

An elder law attorney can provide clients with advice which will vary depending on the laws in place at the time, as well as the client's individual scenario. Resolutions and techniques that are appropriate in Rhode Island may not be appropriate in other states.

By Laura M. Krohn, Attorney at Law, Author

To schedule an appointment with Laura please call:

401-398-8383

Laura M. Krohn Elder Law Attorney
Senior Resource Clinic
631 Main Street
East Greenwich, Rhode Island 02818
www.seniorguideri.com

RI DURABLE POWER OF ATTORNEY: FINANCIAL & REAL ESTATE MATTERS

In many situations, family members or others will need to handle the financial affairs of a loved one. This could range from a single banking transaction to completing a Medicaid application, to selling a house.

To do so, the individual while competent, must have given such person written authority to make decisions on his or her behalf. The usual way this is done is through a document known as a "Durable Power of Attorney". If the Power of Attorney is "Durable" it will continue to be effective even if the person who executed the document becomes incapacitated. The person who signs the Durable Power of Attorney is known as the "principal." The person to whom the power is granted is known as the "agent" or "attorney-in-fact."

A properly drafted Durable Power of Attorney will give the power to gift to the agent, while including language that protects the principal while alive, as well as respects the principal's testamentary objectives.

Failure to execute a Durable Power of Attorney authorizing another to make decisions for you after your incapacity may mean that a court must be asked to appoint someone to assist. This is known as a "guardianship proceeding" and results in substantial legal expense and invasion of privacy.

When choosing an agent, this author always advises clients to choose a person(s) with a strong sense of integrity, who is responsible financially, and who respects and is familiar with the values and objectives of the client. It is a powerful document, which is not reviewed or regulated by any agency. Therefore the potential for abuse by agents under the Power of Attorney is great.

The sufficiency of most Power of Attorney forms is usually tested only after it is too late to make necessary revisions. When having this document prepared for a senior, a professional experienced in elder law issues should be consulted.

By Laura M. Krohn, Attorney at Law, Author

Senior Resource Guide of Rhode Island

To schedule an appointment with Laura please call:

401-398-8383

Laura M. Krohn Elder Law Attorney

Senior Resource Clinic

631 Main Street

East Greenwich, Rhode Island 02818

www.seniorguideri.com

RI DURABLE POWER OF ATTORNEY: HEALTH CARE

An advanced directive is a written document executed by an individual which expresses that individual's health care decisions, including end of life decisions. A health care power of attorney is a document that the individual (referred to as the "Principal") uses to appoint a person (referred to as the "Representative" or "Health Care Agent") to make health decisions in the event the Principal becomes incapacitated. One form can be used for both purposes:

(1) to state a person's advanced health care decisions, and

(2) to appoint a representative.

All states have statutes that deal with a person's ability to make advanced directives. The Rhode Island legislature specifically states that adult persons have the fundamental right to control the decisions relating to the rendering of their own medical care. The Rhode Island legislature also declares the right of an adult person to make a written durable power of attorney for health care decisions and provides a statutory Health Care Power of Attorney form. The Rhode Island statutory Health Care Power of Attorney does provide an opportunity for an individual to state his or her advanced health care decisions.

Many individuals spend all or part of the year in another state, whether for vacation, medical reasons, or to visit family or friends. It is important to know that state laws are not uniform. Therefore, individuals that fall into this category should consider drafting a second health care power of attorney that complies with the law of the second state. Rhode Island recognizes Power of attorneys executed in other states, so long as it is executed in compliance with the laws of that state.

Finally, the choice of a health care representative is a very important decision. The representative should be someone who will honor the Principal's wishes and not be guided by their own wishes. That requires a person who will be emotionally strong and unwavering during times of medical crisis. This author strongly advises that only one health care representative be appointed at a time and always avoid the appointment of joint or co-representatives. The objectives behind executing advanced directives and health care power of attorney documents is to ensure that the health care decisions of the individual executing the document(s) are honored and that litigation is avoided.

By Laura M. Krohn, Attorney at Law, Author

Senior Resource Guide of Rhode Island

To schedule an appointment with Laura please call:

401-398-8383

Laura M. Krohn Elder Law Attorney
Senior Resource Clinic
631 Main Street
East Greenwich, Rhode Island 02818

www.seniorguideri.com

FINANCIAL PLANNING & INSURANCE

THIS CHAPTER IS CONTRIBUTED BY:
EUCLID FINANCIAL SERVICES, LLC
372 BROADWAY, SUITE D
PAWTUCKET, RI 02860
PHONE: (401) 727-2727

WWW.EUCLIDFINANCIALSERVICES.COM
INFO@EUCLIDADVISORS.COM

HOW TO CHOOSE
A FINANCIAL ADVISOR FOR SENIORS

Financial Planning

Choosing an advisor or planner to assist you with your planning can be challenging. However, choosing the financial planner that will take care of the money you worked your whole life to save can be both uncomfortable and frightening.

In this chapter, I will try to provide you with some key information that will make your decisions easier and less stressful, while helping you obtain the best financial planning possible.

Why do I need a Financial Planner?

An experienced financial planner can help assess your needs and objectives, and evaluate the long-term adequacy of your present financial plan in meeting your future goals and needs. If appropriate, they will work with you to find a more suitable long-term plan and develop a retirement portfolio to accommodate this plan. They can also address the burden of estate taxes, in an effort to reduce them, and address the over-all long-term financial benefits.

It is important to note than even if you have a financial planner who has helped you in your pre-retirement years, you may want to seek additional help in your post retirement years. As you retire, financial planning focus may need to shift away from growth and move towards *income* planning, with lower risk involved towards loss. If your pre-retirement planner does not have experience in post-retirement planning, your hard earned retirement savings may not serve you as well as you are anticipating.

How Do I Select a Financial Planner?

While you may receive recommendations from trusted individuals, such as your Elder Law or Estate Attorney or CPA, it is important that you find the financial planner that is right for *you*. This should be someone in whom you have trust and who you are comfortable confiding in.

When interviewing a financial planner to join your retirement team, it may be useful to prepare a set of questions, such as:

- How many years has the planner worked with individuals in their post-retirement years?

- What are their investment philosophies, planning approaches and methods used?

- Do they work independently or are they obligated through a working contractual relationship to give preference to a specific company or product?

- What are their qualifications?

- How much time will be allocated to you?

- What will be the final product to be produced for you?

- How will they be compensated for their services?

Don't be intimidated or afraid to ask questions. An experienced financial planner will be more than willing to take the time to answer any questions you have and understand that it is their responsibility to *earn* your trust. If a planner won't take the time to address your questions or attempts to minimize your concerns, that is not the planner for you.

What can I expect in working with my Financial Planner?

Just as your financial planner needs to take the time to answer your questions, you need to take the time to answer their questions openly and honestly. The planner will help determine what is important for you and what you need to do to accomplish your unique financial plan. You should be able to expect the following from an experienced financial planner:

- A comprehensive assessment of your current financial situation;

- Assistance in helping you determine your financial needs and goals;

- Willingness to work openly with your Estate Planning or Elder Law Attorney and CPA;

- Development of a written financial plan and assistance in its implementation; and

- Creation of a timetable for implementing the plan and helping you periodically review your progress.

Lastly, the individual you select should be understanding and compassionate. However, they should offer you options and alternatives, some of which may be uncomfortable at first, but which may be the most effective way to accomplish your goals. Together, you will be able to create the plan that is right for you.

Joshua J. Wells

Euclid Financial Services LLC

LIFE INSURANCE PLANNING

Life insurance plays an important role in any financial plan, and is a key planning tool for seniors to accomplish their financial goals. In this section we will cover the types of life insurance available to seniors, typical uses for life insurance as you get older, and some key questions to ask when buying any life insurance policy.

There are only 2 main types of life insurance; *Term* and *Permanent*. *Term Life Insurance* is usually thought about as "temporary" life insurance because after the specific term of years passes, the premiums usually become too expensive to maintain the policy. This type of coverage is usually purchased earlier on in life to protect things such as income, mortgage debt, and college planning for children. *Permanent Life Insurance* coverage lasts the entire lifetime of the insured as long as the premiums are paid. Permanent policies also have a "cash value" component which provides accessible funds within the policy. Typically, when planning insurance solutions for seniors, permanent coverage is used and often held in trust to protect it as an asset. We will go into more detail on this strategy later in this section.

Three main variations of permanent coverage are most often used; Traditional Whole Life, Second to Die Whole Life, and Final Expense or Burial Insurance.

Traditional Whole Life Insurance requires the insured to go through a medical and financial underwriting process to determine premiums and how much coverage can be purchased. The more coverage you purchase the more in-depth the underwriting process will be, usually encompassing a medical questionnaire or a sample of blood and urine. However, it may include things such as an EKG, stress test, and full medical physical. Premiums can be paid on a monthly basis, annual basis, or paid with a single premium.

Second-to-Die Life Insurance is a form of whole life coverage used to pass assets to the heirs on the passing of the second insured; no benefit is paid on the passing of the first insured. Medical underwriting is still required; premiums can be paid monthly, annually, or as a single-premium. This type of coverage is usually held in a life insurance trust to minimize taxes in the transfer of the wealth for estate planning purposes.

Final Expense Insurance, **or** *Burial Policies*, requires little to no underwriting, are usually written in amounts of $25,000 or less and solely used to cover burial expenses. These policies can be issued as simplified underwriting (only a few medical questions and no medical exam), or guaranteed issue (meaning no medical questions or exam). Policies can be held in trust or assigned to a funeral home to fund a pre-planned funeral contract.

All three types of permanent coverage, if structured properly, greatly benefit the insured and their families. When combined with estate and trust planning handled by your estate planning attorney, these tools can protect your assets from expensive health and long-term care expenses, as well as maximize the amount passed on to your heirs by leveraging your money and minimizing or avoiding estate taxes.

You may want to consider asking the following key questions when purchasing any type of life insurance coverage. They should assist you in fully understanding the contract in which you are about to enter into.

- How was the amount of coverage determined?

- What type of coverage am I applying for?

- What are the medical underwriting requirements and guidelines?

- Are multiple options being offered to me, or is only one company or product being presented and why?

- Are the premiums guaranteed to stay level over the course of my life?

- What are the potential estate tax concerns with purchasing a policy?

Finally, you should consult your attorney to be sure the product being offered is suitable for your situation.

Raymond J. Dutelle, Jr.

Euclid Financial Services LLC

PRE-PAID FUNERAL FUNDING OPTIONS

You may pay for a pre-paid funeral using a lump sum in cash, by paying in installments, or by using a life insurance policy to leverage your dollars. At most establishments you may also pay in installments to be held in trust. If this is your choice the pre-need contract amount will be upheld, but if you pass before the full amount is paid, your family will be billed for the difference.

Another option to pre-pay for a funeral utilizes permanent life insurance. These are usually issued with simplified underwriting or on a guaranteed-issue basis, meaning little to no medical underwriting is required, and usually offered by a financial professional. A policy may be purchased in lump sum or on an installment plan and may be held personally, held in trust, or assigned to the funeral home to be taken out of the insured's estate. The main reason for using a life insurance policy is to leverage your money to pay less for more services. The amount of leverage would depend on the age at which you purchase the policy. Good questions to ask when purchasing this type of life insurance are; what are the underwriting requirements? Is there a period of time where the full benefit will not be paid? How long will I have to pay into this coverage?

Raymond J. Dutelle, Jr.

Euclid Financial Services LLC

LONG TERM CARE MYTHS

Myth #1: I have no need for long-term care insurance.

Most people don't imagine themselves ever needing long-term care insurance. But, the U.S. Department of Health and Human Services indicates that people age 65 face at least a 40% lifetime risk of entering a nursing home sometime during their lifetime. Living a long life may increase your risk of needing long-term care. Isn't it better to insure against what that risk may do to your family and your financial plans?

Myth #2: Long-term care insurance is something only the elderly need.

Actually, a large amount of long-term care insurance is provided to younger people. The U.S. Government Accountability Office estimates that 40% of 13 million people receiving long-term care services are between the ages 18 and 64. The unexpected need for long-term care could come up at any age for any number of reasons, including illness, or an accident.

Myth #3: I can afford to pay for my own long-term care.

In 2008, the average cost nationally for nursing home care was over $76,400 annually, but in some areas these costs are sometimes twice that amount. How long can you afford to pay for these expenses without endangering your financial plan or exhausting your savings? It may make sense to transfer this risk just like you do with your homeowner's insurance or auto insurance. Even if you can afford to pay for long-term care insurance out of pocket, why would you want to when you can transfer the cost to an insurer for premiums that may total a fraction of the cost of care?

Myth #4: Medicare will cover my long-term care expenses.

Medicare does pay for nursing home care, but only for a maximum of 100 days, and only if the 3-day qualifying hospital stay requirement has been met. In addition, Medicare will only pay as long as you are showing progress towards recovery. Once your condition becomes stable, even if you are not fully well, or back to a completely healthy state of being, Medicare rules indicate that benefits will stop. Also, Medicare does not pay for individuals to attend an adult day care or for the room & board expenses at an assisted living facility.

Myth #5: Medicaid will cover my long-term care expenses.

Medicaid was developed partially to cover long-term care costs for Americans of any age who need help paying for those services. Medicaid is currently the largest payer of long-term care costs in the United States, primarily for care in nursing homes. However, Medicaid focuses on helping people with limited or minimal income and assets. In order to qualify for benefits you must demonstrate a financial need for help. Qualifying for benefits means spending down all of your own assets on your own care before the government will step in to help.

Myth #6: My family will pay for my long-term care needs.

The financial, physical and emotional stress that full-time care-giving may place on families can be overwhelming. Many families have struggled to provide full-time care for parents or siblings only to eventually realize that the care required is more than they can provide. The truth is, sometimes the best way for a family to take care of a loved one needing long-term care is to make sure that they have access to professional care. With the advances in home care services, many people needing long-term care are actually able to stay at home, with or near families, and still get the professional care they need.

Myth #7: Long-term care insurance covers only nursing homes.

Obviously, most people want to stay at home as long as possible. Long-term care insurance can offer valuable benefits that may make that possible. Long-term care insurance can also help cover the cost of care in other locations, such as adult day care centers, assisted living facilities and hospice care.

Raymond J. Dutelle, Jr.

Euclid Financial Services LLC

Notes

WHEN IT IS TIME
TO LEAVE HOME:

WHAT ARE THE OPTIONS?

INDEPENDENT LIVING
ASSISTED LIVING
& NURSING HOME CARE

INDEPENDENT
LIVING

WHAT IS INDEPENDENT LIVING?

Independent Living provides the greatest flexibility and freedom among the many senior housing options available. Independent Living for seniors refers to residence in a compact, easy-to-maintain, private and personal apartment or house within a community of other seniors.

Seniors who decide on Independent Living generally must be healthy and able to manage their homes and personal needs on their own. Those choosing Independent Living simply must have a strong desire to take care of themselves, live independently and be able to communicate with doctors and caregivers on their own.

The housing arrangement is designed exclusively for seniors, generally those aged 55 and older. Typically, services such as meals, activities and transportation are included in a monthly fee. These fees are usually dependent upon the local market. Some subsidized senior Independent Living housing supply financial assistance to those seniors with limited incomes.

Independent Living for seniors is also known as Retirement Communities, Retirement Homes, Senior Apartments, Senior Housing, and Independent Living Communities. It is very important seniors choosing to live independently are willing to reach out for assistance on their own accord.

For additional information regarding the availability at, or amenities of an Independent Living community, call the community's main number and ask for the Director of Community Relations, or for the Admissions Director.

Atria Harborhill

159 Division Street

East Greenwich, RI 02818

www.atriaseniorliving.com

Phone: (401) 884-2704

Fax: (401) 884-2685

The Harborhill community is in a historic mansion that's so awe-inspiring one could spend the entire day walking around marveling at its beauty. The community offers seniors the opportunity to enjoy an independent atmosphere, while receiving assistance as needed with activities of daily living. Atria is committed to catering to the needs of residents and allowing them to maintain independence and dignity. They also offer a secure Life Guidance® neighborhood for seniors.

Greenwich Bay Manor

945 Main Street

East Greenwich, RI 02818

www.horizonbay.com

Phone: (401) 885-3334

Fax: (401) 885-1260

Greenwich Bay Manor offers a variety of spacious, private apartment styles in a cheerful environment that promotes personal independence.

The *Live Well Program* at this community is a comprehensive wellness program designed to provide activities and recreational opportunity, is incorporated into resident care and contains three components: *Activity*, *Forever-Fit* and an *Educational Series*. It encompasses the six dimensions of wellness: physical, intellectual, emotional, social, vocational and spiritual. Greenwich Bay also manages diabetic care for residents which may include glucose monitoring and insulin injections.

Horizon Bay

Supportive Retirement Living   www.horizonbay.com

600 Centre of New England Blvd.   Phone: (401) 821-2445

Coventry, RI 02816   Fax: (401) 821-6180

Horizon Bay's retirement communities create special places for people who want to live in an atmosphere that is calm, comfortable and pleasant. Rich in architectural detail and interior finishes, Horizon Bay makes a grand statement. You will marvel at he variety, spaciousness and high-ceiling drama of their inviting, feature filled apartments.

They'll light up your life with chef-prepared meals, daily housekeeping, fresh linens, chauffeured transportation, wellness programs, a concierge service, and the award winning *Live Well* program. Horizon Bay is committed to helping residents continue living their lives with meaning and purpose. At Horizon Bay, their story is about helping you to continue *your* story.

West Bay Manor

2783 West Shore Road

Warwick, RI 02886

www.horizonbay.com

Phone: (401) 739-7300

Fax: (401) 738-3488

West Bay Manor holds the distinction of being the very first dedicated retirement and assisted living community in all of New England. West Bay Manor is centrally located in the very heart of Rhode Island, minutes from Interstate 95. They offer a variety of independent and assisted living accommodations including eighteen beds dedicated to those with memory impairment. A variety of spacious apartment styles are available to suit individual needs. Many floor plans feature private balconies or patios that look out onto colorful gardens and a private pond.

Greenwich Farms at Warwick

75 Minnesota Avenue

Warwick, RI 02888

www.benchmarkquality.com

Phone: (401) 737-7222

Fax: (401) 737-9702

Greenwich Farms at Warwick is a senior housing community that offers independent living for seniors looking for a carefree lifestyle without the burdens of maintaining a home. They offer a personalized balance of freedom and services seniors need to live well, so that residents can enjoy living exactly as they choose and share new experiences with other community residents celebrating the same wonderful time in their lives. From fine dining and exercise programs, to outings in the area's best cultural attractions, residents can live life exactly as they wish, while their attentive staff takes care of the rest.

Atria Aquidneck Place

125 Quaker Lane

Portsmouth, RI 02871

www.atriaseniorliving.com

Phone: (401) 683-0725

Fax: (401) 683-3072

Atria Aquidneck Place offers the comforts of home and the convenience of shopping and entertainment in nearby historic Newport. They provide the very best in retirement living designed to meet your needs. Aquidneck Place also offers a secure Life Guidance® memory-care neighborhood, the only one of its kind in Rhode Island. The community is located on 5 acres in a quiet, natural setting so you can enjoy life the way you want.

Sakonnet Bay Manor

1215 Main Road

Tiverton, RI 02878

www.horizonbay.com

Phone: (401) 624-1880

Fax: (401) 624-6265

Sakonnet Bay Manor is a premier community located on the site of the former Coachmen Restaurant in Tiverton, RI, near the Fall River, MA, state line. Residents share spectacular sunsets and panoramic vistas in every direction of historic Newport. From independent and assisted living accommodations to the availability of skilled nursing, Sakonnet Bay personalizes all levels of assistance. Sakonnet Bay offers a variety spacious floor plans with the most breathtaking views and a host of modern luxuries: year round swimming in the heated indoor pool, relax in the whirlpool spa, or workout in the fully-equipped Forever Fit exercise and fitness center.

VAA

Emerald Bay Manor

10 Old Diamond Hill Road

Cumberland, RI 02864

www.horizonbay.com

Phone: (401) 333-3393

Fax: (401) 333-6021

Emerald Bay Manor is a community in the quiet country village of Chapel Four Corners in Cumberland, RI, near the Attleboro, MA, state line. At Emerald Bay, quality and tradition combine with an extraordinary array of modern amenities and conveniences. The result is an unsurpassed quality of life, whether that means seeking a completely independent lifestyle, one with assisted living services to make everyday life easier, or the specialized round-the-clock care of a highly skilled nursing.

North Bay Manor

171 Pleasant View Avenue

Smithfield, RI 02917

www.horizonbay.com

Phone: (401) 232-5577

Fax: (401) 232-0225

North Bay Manor, a Horizon Bay community established in 1989, sits amongst rolling hills and spring-fed lakes. North Bay Manor provides the most cheerful independent living accommodations. Enjoy fine dining, arts and crafts, and a host of stimulating and diverse activities that bring new adventures and rewarding opportunities into daily life.

Amenities include a movie theater, 24 hour café, and an outdoor gazebo. The *Live Well Program*, a comprehensive wellness program designed to provide activities and recreational opportunity, is incorporated into resident care. It encompasses the six dimensions of wellness: physical, intellectual, emotional, social, vocational and spiritual.

Capitol Ridge at Providence

700 Smith Street

Providence, RI 02908

www.benchmarkquality.com

Phone: (401) 521-0090

Fax: (401) 453-2514

Capitol Ridge at Providence is a cozy urban retreat situated in historic Providence, overlooking downtown and the State House. The beautiful, historic setting is accented by manicured gardens, private walking paths and gazebos. A terrace off the main dining room offers seasonal outdoor dining with a panoramic view of the neighborhood in all its splendor. Capitol Ridge at Providence offers Independent Living, Assisted Living and the Harbor Program for the Memory Impaired.

   MW

East Bay Manor

1440 Wampanoag Trail

East Providence, RI 02915

www.horizonbay.com

Phone: (401) 433-5000

Fax: (401) 433-4541

Just minutes from Providence, East Bay Manor sits at the gateway to Bristol County and some of the region's most desirable neighborhoods. East Bay offers the most modern conveniences to accommodate many independent lifestyle or ones need for even the most specialized assisted living services. The luxury and convenience of the feature-filled apartments is only the beginning. Outside every door one will enjoy the inviting comfort of richly appointed lounges and dining areas, recreational diversions, and the company and conversation of the friendliest people. The exciting activities and social calendar takes full advantage of East Bay's convenient proximity to a myriad of cultural events and historic sites.

MW VAA

The Villa at St. Antoine Residence   *www.StAntoine.net*

400 Mendon Road   Phone: (401) 767-3500

North Smithfield, RI 02896   Fax: (401) 769-5249

The Villa at St. Antoine offers customized personal care assistance and cultural and social activities. Each apartment offers bright and comfortable living areas, a spacious kitchen and private bath. There are two facilities on their campus. The Villa at St. Antoine has 76 beautiful assisted living apartments, and a wonderful 260 bed nursing facility.

VAA

The Village at Waterman Lake   *www.villageretirement.com*

715 Putnam Pike   Phone: (401) 949-1333

Greenville, RI 02828   Fax: (401) 949-1493

Beautifully landscaped grounds provide the setting for fitness and leisure, including a nine-hole putting green, Bocce court, nature trail, gardens, and greenhouses. The Village interiors combine gracious elegance, homey comfort and practical convenience, all with a remarkable attention to detail. The Village at Waterman Lake offers the perfect blend of hospitality and healthcare, delivered by an expertly trained staff.

Brightview Commons

57 GrandeVille Court

Wakefield, RI 02879

www.brightviewcommons.com

Phone: (401) 789-9777

Fax: (401) 789-3370

Brightview Commons is a wonderfully *uncommon* retirement community. Enjoy independence and freedom from home upkeep in a spacious, 1 or 2 bedroom apartment complete with fully equipped kitchens and washer/dryer. Services include fine dining, housekeeping, 24-hour security, utilities and scheduled transportation - plus-vibrant cultural and educational programs. Brightview Commons is nestled within a quaint, neighborhood village of shops and restaurants in ocean side South County where it feels like vacation every day.

The Elms Assisted Living *www.ElmsAssistedLiving.com*

22 Elm Street Phone: (401) 596-4630

Westerly, RI 02891 Fax: (401) 348-0113

Located in a beautiful residential neighborhood of stately Victorian homes, The Elms is walking distance from historic Wilcox Park and downtown Westerly's unique shops and wonderful restaurants. At The Elms, residents enjoy gourmet meals, complimentary housekeeping, transportation and laundry service. Caregivers are always available to provide assistance if needed. The activities director organizes a wide variety of events both in and out of the community; one more reason the residents and their families agree that The Elms is the perfect solution for those that do not need a nursing home, but may be a little overwhelmed trying to manage things at home.

The Carriage House is the Elms' dedicated community for those with Alzheimer's and other dementia.

South Bay Manor *www.horizonbay.com*

1959 Kingstown Road Phone: (401) 789-4880

South Kingstown, RI 02879 Fax: (401) 792-3780

South Bay Manor is located in the village of Kingston, nestled near the main campus of the University of Rhode Island. South Bay offers a professional staff always ready to help and to prepare meals, clean apartments, or just be a friend. Our affordable, private accommodations and feature-filled floor plans let you live life on ones own terms. Whether it's a day at the beach, exploring a museum, or catching an ocean fresh snack at a seaside restaurant, South County's many resort attractions will keep one busy if desired.

Notes

ASSISTED
LIVING

WHAT IS ASSISTED LIVING?

An assisted living residence provides care for seniors who need some help with activities of daily living yet wish to remain as independent as possible. Essentially, assisted living is the middle ground between independent living and nursing homes. The goal of assisted living is to provide seniors with an environment that encourages as much autonomy as they are capable of, while providing socialization, safety, and family peace of mind. Most residences offer 24-hour supervision and an array of support services, with more privacy, space, and dignity than many nursing homes, and at a lower cost. Assisted Living Residences are also called personal care homes, residential care facilities, domiciliary care, sheltered housing, and community residences.

An Assisted Living Residence helps seniors with personal care/ custodial care, such as bathing, dressing, toileting, eating, grooming and transport. Daily contact with supervisory staff is the defining characteristic of an Assisted Living Residence. Medical care is usually limited in an Assisted Living Residence, but it is possible to contract for other medical needs.

Assisted Living Residences are owned and operated by both for-profit and non-profit organizations and can range in cost depending on where you live. Fees may be inclusive or there may be additional charges for special services.

Costs are generally lower than full-time home health services or nursing home care. Payment options will depend on the individuals situation, and may include private-pay, long-term care insurance, and Medicaid.

For additional information regarding the availability at, or amenities of an Assisted Living community, call the community's main number and ask for the Director of Community Relations, or for the Admissions Director.

Atria Harborhill

159 Division Street

East Greenwich, RI 02818

www.AtriaSeniorLiving.com

Phone: (401) 884-2704

Fax: (401) 884-2685

The Harborhill community is in a historic mansion that's so awe-inspiring one could spend the entire day walking around marveling at its beauty. The community offers seniors the opportunity to enjoy an independent atmosphere, while receiving assistance as needed with activities of daily living. Atria is committed to catering to the needs of residents and allowing them to maintain independence and dignity. They also offer a secure Life Guidance® neighborhood for seniors.

Greenwich Bay Manor

945 Main Street

East Greenwich, RI 02818

www.HorizonBay.com

Phone: (401) 885-3334

Fax: (401) 885-1260

Greenwich Bay Manor offers a variety of spacious, private apartment styles in a cheerful environment that promotes personal independence.

The *Live Well Program* at this community is a comprehensive wellness program designed to provide activities and recreational opportunity, is incorporated into resident care and contains three components: *Activity*, *Forever-Fit* and an *Educational Series*. It encompasses the six dimensions of wellness: physical, intellectual, emotional, social, vocational and spiritual. Greenwich Bay also manages diabetic care for residents which may include glucose monitoring and insulin injections.

wich Farms at Warwick   www.benchmarkquality.com

,ɔ Minnesota Avenue   Phone: (401) 737-7222

Warwick, RI 02888   Fax: (401) 737-9702

Greenwich Farms at Warwick is a senior housing community that offers a personalized balance of assistance and independence. Enjoy the privacy of your own apartment and the support of their caring staff for anything you may need, from personal care and transportation, to medication and continence management, or even just a friend to check in and chat.

You will receive the assistance you want and need from their full continuum of personal care services, provided in the comfort and privacy of your own apartment. This Benchmark community offers different plans, ensuring that you receive the care that fits into your lifestyle.

New England Bay *Brookdale*

Supportive Retirement Living   www.horizonbay.com

600 Centre of New England Blvd.   Phone: (401) 821-2445

Coventry, RI 02816   Fax: (401) 821-6180

They'll light up your life with chef-prepared meals, daily housekeeping, fresh linens, chauffeured transportation, wellness programs, a concierge service, and the award winning *Live Well* program. Horizon Bay is committed to helping residents continue living their lives with meaning and purpose.

Horizon Bay's *Memory Care Neighborhood* is designed to create pleasant days in what can seem like a confusing world. They offer your loved one a calm and predictable lifestyle by focusing on each resident as the center of the care process-honoring their unique life experiences and personalities. Horizon Bay is committed to helping residents continue living their lives with meaning and purpose. At Horizon Bay, their story is about helping you to continue *your* story.

The Seasons East Greenwich

5 Saint Elizabeth Way

East Greenwich, RI 02818

www.TheSeasons.org

Phone: (401) 884-9099

401 884-9077

Fax: (401) 884-7439

The Seasons East Greenwich is a non-profit assisted living and memory-impaired residence founded by the Scandinavian Home and Steere House Nursing and Rehabilitation Center. The residence offer 64 private, unfurnished studio, one bedroom and two bedroom apartments with private bath and kitchenette for traditional assisted living residents. Grandview Gardens, the community for those with Alzheimer's disease or other memory impairments, offer 20 private studio apartments with private bath. Residents are offered a full range of assisted living services including three meals daily, bathing and dressing assistance, medication administration, and housekeeping and laundry. Activities are scheduled daily to enhance residents' independence and social, recreational, cultural, physical and spiritual needs, Through The Seasons founding members and associations, they are able to offer priority admission to some of the state's finest nursing homes.

Summer Villa

51 Laurel Avenue

Coventry, RI 02816

Phone: (401) 828-8280

Fax: (401) 828-8283

Summer Villa is a private, family owned assisted living residence since 2002. The Villa offers individuals an independent lifestyle with assistance as needed.

VAA

The Phyllis Siperstein Tamarisk Assisted Living   *www.TamariskRI.org*

3 Shalom Drive

Warwick, RI 02886

Phone: (401) 732-0037

Fax: (401) 921-0602

Tamarisk, developed by the Jewish Seniors Agency of RI, is the only kosher assisted living community in the state. This New England style residence, with covered porches, courtyards, gardens and walking paths, welcomes residents with the warmth of home and places strong emphasis on culture and the arts. Tamarisk offers specialized care to residents with Alzheimer's disease and other forms of memory impairment through the *Renaissance Memory Support Program* which occupies a specially designed and dedicated wing. This wing contains a state of the art "Snoezelen Room" which was developed to satisfy perceptual needs of people with learning or sensory disabilities and provides stimulation and relaxation through the use of smell, touch, sound, color and light. Tamarisk welcomes all seniors without regard to religious affiliation.

West Bay Manor

2783 West Shore Road

Warwick, RI 02886

www.horizonbay.com

Phone: (401) 739-7300

Fax: (401) 738-3488

West Bay Manor holds the distinction of being the very first dedicated retirement and assisted living community in all of New England. West Bay Manor is centrally located in the very heart of Rhode Island. They offer a variety of independent and assisted living accommodations including 18 beds dedicated to those with memory impairment. A variety of spacious apartment styles are available to suit individual needs. Many floor plans feature private balconies or patios that look out onto colorful gardens and a private pond. Among the various amenities at West Bay are a therapeutic spa and theater. Diabetic care is available to residents. The *Live Well Program*, a comprehensive wellness program designed to provide activities and recreational opportunity, is incorporated into resident care. It encompasses the six dimensions of wellness: physical, intellectual, emotional, social, vocational and spiritual.

Atria Aquidneck Place   *www.AtriaSeniorLiving.com*

125 Quaker Lane   Phone: (401) 683-0725

Portsmouth, RI 02871   Fax: (401) 683-3072

Atria Aquidneck Place offers the comforts of home and the convenience of shopping and entertainment in nearby historic Newport. They provide the very best in retirement living designed to meet your needs. Aquidneck Place also offers a secure Life Guidance® memory-care neighborhood, the only one of its kind in Rhode Island. The community is located on 5 acres in a quiet, natural setting so you can enjoy life the way you want.

Blenheim-Newport   *www.BenchmarkQuality.com*

303 Valley Road   Phone: (401) 849-0031

Middletown, RI 02842   Fax: (401) 849-0199

Blenheim-Newport is a fairly new Benchmark Senior Living Community, established in early 2007. Newly renovated and situated on fifteen beautiful acres, Blenheim-Newport borders historic Newport, offering many cultural, educational and recreational opportunities. The assisted living program promotes a lifestyle that combines all the services and amenities of independent living with the convenience of health services and assistance offered in the privacy of ones own apartment. Within the community is a specially designed program for the memory impaired. The safe and secure environment in *The Harbor Program* offers specially designed programs to accommodate people with dementia.

Sakonnet Bay Manor   *www.HorizonBay.com*

1215 Main Road   Phone: (401) 624-1880

Tiverton, RI 02878   Fax: (401) 624-6264

Sakonnet Bay Manor, a Horizon Bay community, is perched high above Mt.Hope Bay and lends residents spectacular views of historic Newport, moonlit bridges and one of New England's most scenic waterways. In addition to breathtaking views, Sakonnet Bay offers its residents a heated indoor pool, a whirlpool spa and a fully-equipped exercise and fitness center. A pub and movie theater are also available. The *Live Well Program*, a comprehensive wellness program designed to provide activities and recreational opportunity, is incorporated into resident care.

VAA

If you are interested in purchasing an extra copy, please visit us at *www.seniorguideri.com* *or call (401) 398-8383*

Ashberry Manor

1081 Mineral Spring Avenue   Phone: (401) 728-8500

North Providence, RI 02904   Fax: (401) 722-4705

Ashberry Manor, established in 1999, is a privately owned assisted living residence. The Manor offers residents a warm, cozy, home-like atmosphere. Because of its small size, attention is highly individualized and each resident quickly becomes part of a family along with the other residents and staff. Ashberry Manor is closely situated near many religious services.

Capitol Ridge at Providence

700 Smith Street

Providence, RI 02908

www.benchmarkquality.com

Phone: (401) 521-0090

Fax: (401) 453-2514

Capitol Ridge at Providence, a Benchmark community, is a cozy urban retreat situated in historic Providence, overlooking downtown and the State House. The beautiful, historic setting is accented by manicured gardens, private walking paths and gazebos. A terrace off the main dining room offers seasonal outdoor dining with a panoramic view of the neighborhood in all its splendor. Capitol Ridge at Providence offers Independent Living, Assisted Living and The Harbor Program for the Memory Impaired.

 MW

Darlington Assisted Living

123 Armistice Boulevard   Phone: (401) 725-2400

Pawtucket, RI 02860   Fax: (401) 724-8722

Darlington, established in 1980, is a privately owned assisted living residence. The Residence offers residents a warm, cozy, home-like atmosphere. Because of its small size, attention is highly individualized and each resident quickly becomes part of a family along with the other residents and staff. This residency is equipped with a wanderguard system to handle memory impaired individuals.

Darlington Assisted Living II

56 Maynard Street   Phone: (401) 725-0700

Pawtucket, RI 02860   Fax: (401) 724-8240

Darlington II, established in 1997, is a privately owned assisted living residence. The Manor offers residents a warm, cozy, home-like atmosphere. Because of its small size, attention is highly individualized and each resident quickly becomes part of a family along with the other residents and staff. No private rooms are available.

MW   VAA

East Bay Manor

1440 Wampanoag Trail   *www.horizonbay.com*

East Providence, RI 02915   Phone: (401) 433-5000

                                         Fax: (401) 433-4541

Just minutes from Providence, East Bay Manor sits at the gateway to Bristol County and some of the region's most desirable neighborhoods. East Bay offers the most modern conveniences to accommodate many independent lifestyle or ones need for even the most specialized assisted living services. Outside every door one will enjoy the inviting comfort of richly appointed lounges and dining areas, recreational diversions, and the company and conversation of the friendliest people. The exciting activities and social calendar takes full advantage of East Bay's convenient proximity to a myriad of cultural events and historic sites.

Emerald Bay Manor

www.horizonbay.com

10 Old Diamond Hill Road

Phone: (401) 333-3393

Cumberland, RI 02864

Fax: (401) 333-6021

Emerald Bay Manor, a Horizon Bay community, is situated in the quiet country village of Chapel Four Corners near the Massachusetts state line. The amenities include a heated indoor pool as well as a relaxing spa. Among a wide range of activities, Emerald Bay offers painting and piano lessons. The *Live Well Program*, a comprehensive wellness program designed to provide activities and recreational opportunity, is incorporated into resident care. It encompasses the six dimensions of wellness: physical, intellectual, emotional, social, vocational and spiritual.

North Bay Manor

www.horizonbay.com

171 Pleasant View Avenue

Phone: (401) 232-5577

Smithfield, RI 02917

Fax: (401) 232-0225

North Bay Manor, a Horizon Bay community established in 1989, sits amongst rolling hills and spring-fed lakes. Assisted living services are tailored to residents' specific needs. Amenities include a movie theater, 24 hour café, and an outdoor gazebo. The *Live Well Program*, a comprehensive wellness program designed to provide activities and recreational opportunity, is incorporated into resident care. It encompasses the six dimensions of wellness: physical, intellectual, emotional, social, vocational and spiritual.

Saint Elizabeth Court

www.StElizabethCommunity.com

109 Melrose Street

Phone: (401) 490-4646

Providence, RI 02907

Fax: (401) 490-4537

Saint Elizabeth Court, a member of the Saint Elizabeth Community, is an assisted living residence for seniors, located in the heart of historic Elmwood. Housed in a beautiful turn-of-the-century building, The Court offers the charm of yesteryear with the appeal of modern conveniences. Amenities include a beautifully landscaped courtyard, enclosed porch and chapel.

Tockwotton Home

www.Tockwotton.org

75 East Street

Phone: (401) 272-5280

Providence, RI 02903

Fax: (401) 421-0550

Tockwotton Home, established in 1856, is a non-profit assisted living residence. It is located in the heart of Rhode Island, in a lovely Victorian style building, furnished with antiques, oil paintings and china cabinets. Nursing services and personal care services are based on individual need and preference.

The Willows Assisted Living

www.rhodeislandnursing.com

47 Barker Avenue

Phone: (401) 245-2323

Warren, RI 02919

Fax: (401) 247-9030

Since 1966 The Willows has been serving those in the East Bay. Our assisted living residence, nestled in a quiet residential area along the Kickemuit River, provides our residents with generously-sized suites in either studio or 1-bedroom designs. Our services and amenities include medication administration, meals, housekeeping, scheduled transportation and 24-hour certified staff.

The Villa at Saint Antoine

400 Mendon Road

North Smithfield, RI 02896

www.StAntoine.net

Phone: (401) 767-2574

Fax: (401) 767-2581

The Villa at Saint Antoine is a non profit assisted living facility, an agency of the Catholic Diocese of Providence, offering a variety of supported services to their Residents. Some of these services include daily mass and rosary, transportation, housekeeping and lien services medication monitoring and 24-hour nursing care. The Villa offers gracious French country interiors, with beautifully landscaped grounds and gardens. Residents have priority access to Saint Antoine Residence which is located on the same campus, for short-term rehabilitation or long-term care.

VAA

The Village at Waterman Lake

715 Putnam Pike

Greenville, RI 02828

www.villageretirement.com

Phone: (401) 949-1333

Fax: (401) 949-1493

Beautifully landscaped grounds provide the setting for fitness and leisure, including a nine-hole putting green, Bocce court, nature trail, gardens, and greenhouses. The Village interiors combine gracious elegance, homey comfort and practical convenience, all with a remarkable attention to detail. The Village at Waterman Lake offers the perfect blend of hospitality and healthcare, delivered by an expertly trained staff.

Brightview Commons

www.BrightviewCommons

57 GrandeVille Court

Wakefield, RI 02879

Phone: (401) 789-9777
401.789.8777

Fax: (401) 789-3370

Located in South Kingstown, Rhode Island, Brightview Commons, serves Wakefield, Narragansett, Providence and surrounding areas. It is one of the newest active rental retirement communities in the South County area and is honored to offer Independent Living, Assisted Living, and Wellspring Village, a special care program for those with Alzheimer's Disease or other forms of memory impairment. With a choice of apartment homes, the goal at Brightview Commons is to accommodate their residents in experiencing life as they choose.

South Bay Manor

www.horizonbay.com

1959 Kingstown Road

South Kingstown, RI 02879

Phone: (401) 789-4880

Fax: (401) 792-3780

South Bay Manor, a Horizon Bay Community, is nestled near the main campus of University of Rhode Island. South County's many resort attractions are just minutes away. The *Live Well! Program*, a comprehensive wellness program designed to provide activities and recreational opportunity, is incorporated into resident care. It encompasses the six dimensions of wellness: physical, intellectual, emotional, social, vocational and spiritual.

The Elms

22 Elm Street

Westerly, RI 02891

www.ElmsAssistedLiving.com

Phone: (401) 596-4630

Fax: (401) 348-0113

The Elms, established in 1985, is located in a beautiful residential neighborhood of stately Victorian homes. It is walking distance from historic Wilcox Park and the downtown area. The *Carriage House* at The Elms is a dedicated special care community for individuals with early-stage Alzheimer's and dementia. Specialized daily activities promotes positive purpose in a specially designed environment that includes walking paths and gardens in a secure setting.

Notes

Notes

NURSING HOMES
& REHABILITATION

WHAT IS A NURSING HOME & REHABILITATION CENTER?

A Nursing Home provides 24 hour care to people who can no longer care for themselves due to physical, emotional, or mental conditions. A licensed physician supervises each patient's care and a nurse or other medical professional is almost always on the premises. Most nursing homes have two basic types of services: skilled medical care and custodial care.

Skilled medical care includes services of trained professionals that are needed for a limited period of time following an injury or illness. This may include would care, I.V. administration and monitoring, physical therapy, speech therapy, occupational therapy, or administering and monitoring I.V. antibiotics for a severe infection. Skilled care may also be needed on a long term basis if a resident requires injections, ventilation or other similar treatment.

Custodial or personal care includes assistance with what are known as the activities of daily living. These include bathing, dressing, eating, grooming, transport, and incontinence care. This type of care may be a temporary or long-term need depending on the situation.

Nursing Homes/Skilled Nursing Facilities offer an array of services, in addition to the basic skilled nursing care and the custodial care. They provide a room (private or semi-private), all meals, some social activities, personal care, 24-hour nursing supervision and access to medical services when needed. In addition, many Nursing Homes provide respite care so that caregivers can have a break, and interim medical care which is care after a hospital stay.

Rhode Island Veterans Home

480 Metacom Avenue

Bristol, RI 02809

www.dhs.state.ri.us

Phone: (401) 253-8000

Fax: (401) 254-8365

The Rhode Island Veterans Home, a 110-acre complex located on Mount Hope Bay. The mission of the home is to provide quality nursing and residential care to those Rhode Island war veterans in need. Social, medical, nursing and rehabilitative services are also provided to veterans and their survivors and/or dependents to improve their physical, emotional and economic well-being. The Veterans Home consists of 260 nursing care beds in three skilled and semiskilled units and two ambulatory care units and two ambulatory care units with an additional 79 beds.

Silver Creek Manor

7 Creek Lane

Bristol, RI 02809

www.SilverCreekManor.com

Phone: (401) 253-3000

Fax: (401) 254-1289

Saint Elizabeth Manor

1 Dawn Hill

Bristol, RI 02809

www.stelizabethcommunity.com

Phone: (401) 253-2300

Fax: (401) 254-1919

Saint Elizabeth Manor, a non-profit nonsectarian charitable organization, has a long history of providing quality care in the East Bay. Short-term rehabilitation, long-term nursing, and specialized Alzheimer's care are services provided by experienced, trained staff. The Manor, home to 133 women and men, is situated in a picturesque, residential setting. Recognizing individual preferences and routines is central to the care model.

R

Crestwood Nursing & Convalescent Home

568 Child Street   Phone: (401) 245-1574

Warren, RI 02885   Fax: (401) 247-0211

Grace Barker Nursing Center

54 Barker Avenue   Phone: (401) 245-9100

Warren, RI 02885   Fax: (401) 245-3730

Since 1966 Grace Barker Nursing Center has been serving those in the East Bay. They offer long term care, rehabilitation services, restorative care, Alzheimer's/dementia , and family support. The campus, housing both Grace Barker Nursing Center and The Willows Assisted Living and Adult Day Community, affords one the advantage of continuity of care at one location. A familiar environment of friends and surroundings allows a smooth transition from one service to another.

Haven Health Center of Warren

642 Metacom Avenue   Phone: (401) 245-2860

Warren, RI 02885   Fax: (401) 245-0959

Alpine Nursing Home

557 Weaver Hill Road

Coventry, RI 02816

Phone: (401) 397-5001

Fax: (401) 397-2455

Brentwood Nursing Home

4000 Post Road

Warwick, RI 02886

R

www.BrentwoodNursingHome.com

Phone: (401) 884-8020

Fax: (401) 884-7977

Harborside Healthcare Greenwood

1139 Main Avenue

Warwick, RI 02886

www.HarborsideHealthcare.com

Phone: (401) 739-6600

Fax: (401) 738-0310

Serving 134 residents, Harborside Healthcare Greenwood provides care and services for patients recovering from a variety of concerns including cardiac recovery, diabetes management, dialysis management, and orthopedic rehabilitation.

R

Haven Health Center of Coventry

10 Woodland Drive

Coventry, RI 02816

www.HavenHealthCare.com

Phone: (401) 826-2000

Fax: (401) 821-0260

Haven Health Center of Coventry, serving up to 210 residents, includes specialized units rehab, long-term care and dementia care. Our rehabilitation program advances the success of patients returning to home with our newly renovated simulated home entertainment. Our long-term suites accommodate both higher functioning residents as well as those that require additional care. The secured Dementia unit specializes in geriatric care and needs of this population. We also collaborate with local Hospice agencies.

Riverview Healthcare Community

546 Main Street

Coventry, RI 02816

R

Phone: (401) 821-6837

Fax: (401) 823-9840

Saint Elizabeth Home

1 Saint Elizabeth Way

East Greenwich, RI 02818

www.StElizabethCommunity.com

Phone: (401) 471-6060

Fax: (401) 471-6072

The Saint Elizabeth Home is a non-profit nursing residence for 120 men and women and a member of the Saint Elizabeth Community. Saint Elizabeth Home offers both nursing and rehabilitative care, along with a secure, special care living area for individuals with Alzheimer's and/or dementia. A hospice team provides end of life care. They opened in Providence in 1882, and moved into a brand new residence in East Greenwich in 2001. The secure Alzheimer's/dementia care space has a beautiful secure garden complete with sitting areas, an arbor, and brook.

R

Sunny View Nursing Home

83 Corona Street

Warwick, RI 02886

Phone: (401) 737-9193

Fax: (401) 737-9196

West Shore Health Center

109 West Shore Road

Warwick, RI 02889

www.HCLTDRI.com

Phone: (401) 739-9440

Fax: (401) 921-2687

West View Healthcare Center

239 Legris Avenue

West Warwick, RI 02893

www.WestViewNursing.com

Phone: (401) 828-9000

Fax: (401) 828-7640

Forest Farm Healthcare Centre   *www.ForestFarmHealthcare.com*

193 Forest Avenue   Phone: (401) 847-2777

Middletown, RI 02842   Fax: (401) 848-7403

Forest Farm Health Care Center has been providing services to the Aquidneck Island community since 1932. Located in a rural setting in Middletown, Rhode Island, this modern facility was constructed in 1975 and was designed to meet all state and federal standards for a health care facility. Forest Farm has continued to expand to meet the ever-changing health care needs of the community. The Adult Day Care, Assisted Living, and NewCare provide elders and their families quality support at different levels of care.

Grand Islander Center

333 Green End Avenue   Phone: (401) 849-7100

Middletown, RI 02840   Fax: (401) 849-6076

Heatherwood Nursing & Rehabilitation Center

www.heatherwoodnursing.com

398 Bellevue Avenue   Phone: (401) 849-6600

Newport, RI 02840   Fax: (401) 845-6969

HMS of Newport, doing business as Heatherwood Nursing & Nursing Center in beautiful historic Newport, RI is all about you. There's nothing more cherished than the residents health and independence. To be free to do the things residents like to do. At HMS of Newport, their dedicated to helping patients who suffer from an illness or an injury return home to their independent lifestyles as quickly as possible. With HMS Rehabilitation Care Services, our patients receive comprehensive care and support from our compassionate staff as they make their transition home.

The John Clarke Retirement Center   *www.JohnClarke.org*

600 Valley Road   Phone: (401) 846-0743

Middletown, RI 02842   Fax: (401) 367-0090

Sakonnet Bay Manor   *www.HorizonBay.com*

1215 Main Road   Phone: (401) 624-1880

Tiverton, RI 02878   Fax: (401) 624-6265

St. Clare's Home for the Aged   *www.StClareHome.com*

309 Spring Street   Phone: (401) 849-3204

Newport, RI 02840   Fax: (401) 849-5780

Saint Clare Home is a 47-bed skilled nursing facility nestled in the heart
of downtown Newport. As a health care agency of the Roman Catholic
Diocese of Providence, Saint Clare Home serves the needs of individuals
with varied health issues and diagnoses. These services include skilled
and non-skilled nursing care provided 24 hours per day by a trained and
educated staff.

R

Village House Convalescent Home

70 Harrison Avenue   Phone: (401) 849-5222

Newport, RI 02840   Fax: (401) 849-5765

R

If you are interested in purchasing an extra
copy, please visit us at
www.seniorguideri.com
or call (401) 398-8383

Ballou Home for the Aged

60 Mendon Road

Woonsocket, RI 02895

Phone: (401) 769-0437

Fax: (401) 769-7481

Bannister House

135 Dodge Street

Providence, RI 02907

Phone: (401) 521-9600

Fax: (401) 274-3233

R

Bayberry Commons

181 Davis Drive

Pascoag, RI 02859

Phone: (401) 568-0600

Fax: (401) 568-3080

Berkshire Place

455 Douglas Avenue

Providence, RI 02908

Phone: (401) 553-8600

Fax: (401) 553-8608

R

R

Bethany Home of Rhode Island

111South Angell Street

Providence, RI 02906

Phone: (401) 831-2870

Fax: (401) 331-9570

R

Briarcliffe Manor

www.BriarcliffeManor.com

44 Old Pocasset Road

Johnston, RI 02919

Phone: (401) 944-2450

Fax: (401) 944-2455

Briarcliffe Manor is a privately owned, 122 bed nursing and rehabilitation center set on 20 acres of beautiful, wooded land.

R

Charlesgate Nursing Center

100 Randall Street

Providence, RI 02904

Phone: (401) 861-5858

Fax: (401) 861-2540

Cherry Hill Manor

2 Cherry Hill Road

Johnston, RI 02919

Phone: (401) 231-3102

Fax: (401) 232-5520

Cedar Crest Nursing Centre

125 Scituate Avenue

Cranston, RI 02921

Phone: (401) 944-8500

Fax: (401) 944-5162

Cra-Mar Meadows

575 Seven Mile Road

Cranston, RI 02920

Phone: (401) 828-5010

Fax: (401) 828-0616

Eastgate Nursing & Recovery Center

198 Waterman Avenue

East Providence, RI 02914

R

Phone: (401) 431-2087

Fax: (401) 435-6465

Elmhurst Extended Care Facility

50 Maude Street

Providence, RI 02908

R

www.ElmhurstExtendedCare.org

Phone: (401) 456-2600

Fax: (401) 456-6473

Elmwood Health Center

225 Elmwood Avenue

Providence, RI 02907

Phone: (401) 272-0600

Fax: (401) 454-0818

Emerald Bay Manor

10 Old Diamond Hill Road

Cumberland, RI 02864

www.HorizonBay.com

Phone: (401) 333-3393

Fax: (401) 333-6021

Emerald Bay Manor is a community in the village of Chapel Four Corners in Cumberland, RI, near the Attleboro, MA, state line. At Emerald Bay, part of the Horizon Bay Senior Communities, quality and tradition combine with an array of modern amenities and conveniences. Whether residents seek a completely independent lifestyle, or one with assisted living services to make everyday life easier, or require the specialized round-the-clock care of a highly skilled nursing center.

The Friendly Home, Inc.

303 Rhodes Avenue

Woonsocket, RI 02985

Phone: (401) 769-7220

Fax: (401) 766-8282

The Friendly Home has been serving the community for over 40 years. Each resident is valued as an individual with his or her own needs for privacy, dignity and individualized care. 24 hour skilled care is available as well as intermediate care.

R

Evergreen House Health Center

1 Evergreen Drive

East Providence, RI 02914

www.LCCA.com

Phone: (401) 438-3250

Fax: (401) 438-4813

Epoch Senior Healthcare on Blackstone Boulevard

353 Blackstone Boulevard

Providence, RI 02906

www.EpochSL.com

Phone: (401) 273-6565

Fax: (401) 273-6568

Grandview Center

100 Chambers Street

Cumberland, RI 02864

Phone: (401) 724-7500

Fax: (401) 724-7543

Hallworth House

66 Benefit Street

Providence, RI 02904

www.episcopalri.org

Phone: (401) 274-4505

Fax: (401) 521-3947

Golden Crest Nursing Centre

100 Smithfield Road

N. Providence, RI 02904

Phone: (401) 353-1710

Fax: (401) 353-1618

Harris Health Care Center North

60 Eben Brown Lane

Central Falls, RI 02863

R

www.HarrisHealth.com/hhcn.htm

Phone: (401) 722-6000

Fax: (401) 726-0850

Hattie Ide Chaffee Home

200 Wampanoag Trail

East Providence, RI 02914

Phone: (401) 434-1520

Fax: (401) 438-8494

Harris Health Center

833 Broadway

East Providence, RI 02914

R

www.HarrisHealth.com

Phone: (401) 434-7404

Fax: (401) 435-4255

Haven Health Center of Greenville   *www.havenhealthcare.com*

735 Putnam Pike   Phone: (401) 949-1200

Greenville, RI 02828   Fax: (401) 949-1204

Haven Health Center of Pawtucket   *www.havenhealthcare.com*

70 Gill Avenue   Phone: (401) 722-7900

Pawtucket, RI 02861   Fax: (401) 723-9670

Hebert's Nursing Home

180 Log Road   Phone: (401) 231-7016

Smithfield, RI 02917   Fax: (401) 231-4018

Heritage Hills Nursing Centre

80 Douglas Pike   Phone: (401) 231-2700

Smithfield, RI 02917   Fax: (401) 231-2703

R

Hopkins Manor, Ltd.   *www.HopkinsManor.com*

610 Smithfield Road   Phone: (401) 353-6300

N. Providence, RI 02904   Fax: (401) 353-8165

Kindred Heights Nursing & Rehab Center

100 Wampanoag Trail   Phone: (401) 438-4275

Riverside, RI 02915   Fax: (401) 438-8093

Linn Health Care Center

30 Alexander Avenue

Phone: (401) 438-7210

East Providence, RI 02914

Fax: (401) 435-4231

R

The Mansion Nursing Home

www.MansionNursing.com

104 Clay Street

Phone: (401) 722-0830

Central Falls, RI 02863

Fax: (401) 728-1814

Established in 1948, The Mansion Nursing Home, a family owned facility, provides an individualized care plan which is delivered upon admission and updated quarterly. A highly qualified staff provides residents with the highest level of care and through a varied recreational, cultural, and motivational activities program the Mansion aims to keep their residents engaged and interested in their daily lives while giving them the comfort and familiarity to reflect.

Morgan Health Center

80 Morgan Avenue

Phone: (401) 944-7800

Johnston, RI 02919

Fax: (401) 944-6037

R

Mount St. Francis Health Center

4 Saint Joseph Street

Phone: (401) 765-5844

Woonsocket, RI 02895

Fax: (401) 762-2015

Chestnut Terrace

15 Sumner Brown Road

Phone: (401) 333-6352

Cumberland, RI 02864

Fax: (401) 333-1012

Nancy Ann Nursing Home

48 East Killingly Road

Foster, RI 02825

Phone: (401) 647-2170

Fax: (401) 647-9020

R

North Bay Manor

171 Pleasant View Avenue

Smithfield, RI 02917

www.HorizonBay.com

Phone: (401) 232-5577

Fax: (401) 232-0225

On a peninsula surrounded by the waters of a nearby spring-fed lake sits North Bay Manor, a community where a relaxing lifestyle is in perfect harmony with nature. At North Bay Manor, a complete continuum of care includes independent living accommodations, assisted living services tailored to personal needs, and the advanced care offered by a fully-licensed skilled nursing center. North Bay offers fine dining, arts and crafts, and a host of stimulating and diverse activities.

Oak Hill Nursing & Rehab Center

544 Pleasant Street

Pawtucket, RI 0286

Phone: (401) 725-8888

Fax: (401) 727-8795

Oakland Grove Health Care Center

560 Cumberland Hill Road

Woonsocket, RI 02895

www.AthenaHealthcare.com/og.htm

Phone: (401) 769-0800

Fax: (401) 766-3661

Orchard View Manor Nursing & Rehabilitation Center

135 Tripps Lane   *www.OrchardViewManor.com*

East Providence, RI 02915   Phone: (401) 438-2250

                                   Fax: (401) 438-0635

Since 1977, Orchard View Manor's interdisciplinary approach to sub-acute rehabilitation and long term care helps individuals with impairments resulting from stroke, amputation, trauma, injury or neurological disease and/or joint replacement. Their sub-acute program utilizes the services of psychiatrists, podiatrists, urologists, dentists, optometrists, surgeons and dermatologists for the treatment of cancer, cardiac and pulmonary disease or other medically complex conditions. Programs encompass specialized medical and nursing management, on-site physical, occupational and speech therapy, case management, and discharge planning services. Facility pets create a homelike environment.

R

Park View Nursing Home

31 Parade Street   Phone: (401) 351-2600

Providence, RI 02909   Fax: (401) 421-0183

Scandinavian Home

1811 Broad Street   *www.ScandinavianHome.com*

                                   Phone: (401) 461-1433

Cranston, RI 02905   Fax: (401) 461-4005

Summit Commons

99 Hillside Avenue   www.radiushealthcarecenters.com

                                   Phone: (401) 574-4800

Providence, RI 02906   Fax: (401) 278-4937

R

Pine Grove Health & Sub-Acute Center

999 South Main Street

Pascoag, RI 02859

Phone: (401) 568-3091

Fax: (401) 568-8070

Pine Grove Health Center is situated in a tranquil country setting. It is organized with a commitment to provide excellence in sub-acute, skilled and long-term care. Services involve the expertise of the medical, nursing, rehabilitative, dietary, social service, and activity staffs.

R

Saint Antoine Residence

www.StAntoine.net / residence.htm

10 Rhodes Avenue

N. Smithfield, RI 02896

Phone: (401) 767-3500

Fax: (401) 769-5249

Saint Antoine Residence, established in 1913, is a nursing and rehabilitation center that is sponsored by the Diocese of Providence. The Residence offers skilled nursing beds with a special care unit for individuals with Alzheimer's and related dementia. The Residence adheres to the Diocesan mission and long tradition of caring for the sick and the elderly. Also included on the Saint Antoine campus is a sub-cute transitional care unit.

Steere House Nursing & Rehab Center

www.steerehoues.org

100 Borden Street

Providence, RI 02903

Phone: (401) 454-7970

Fax: (401) 831-7570

Since 1874, Steere House has been an independent non-profit organization, serving adults who require skilled, restorative, and long-term care services within a secure and caring environment. Steere House also provides educational and research experiences that enhance the care of those they serve. Steere house has one of the best staff resident ratios in the state, provides short-term rehabilitation, Mid and Late Stage Alzheimer's Disease and Dementia Care, and offers an extensive program of leisure and therapeutic recreation.

Tockwotton Home

75 East Street

Providence, RI 02903

www.Tockwotton.org

Phone: (401) 272-5280

Fax: (401) 421-0550

Tockwotton Home is a non-profit nursing and assisted living residence. It is located in the heart of Rhode Island, in a lovely Victorian style building, furnished with antiques. Nursing services and personal care services are based on individual need and preference. This home was established in 1856 and is very unique.

Woodland Convalescent Center

70 Woodland Road

Phone: (401) 765-0499

Woonsocket Health Centre

262 Poplar Street

Woonsocket, RI 02895

Phone: (401) 765-2100

Fax: (401) 232-7275

Waterview Villa Nursing & Rehabilitation Center

1275 South Broadway

Providence, RI 02914

Secure Unit/Rehabilitation

www.WaterviewVilla.com.

Phone: (401) 438-7020

Fax: (401) 438-0013

Roberts Health Centre

www.RobertsHealthCentre.com

25 Roberts Way

Phone: (401) 294-3587

N. Kingstown, RI 02852

Fax: (401) 295-9357

Robert's Health Centre is proud to be one of Rhode Island's premiere skilled nursing homes since 1982. Roberts Health Centre is a family operated Health Centre with a focus on providing the very best in individual rehabilitation care and nursing for up to 66 residents. Their unique Rehab and Nursing facility is nestled in the town of Wickford, North Kingstown amid the ocean breeze. Robert's offers both short term and long-term care to residents who meet skilled or intermediate level of care criteria. R

Scalabrini Villa

www.ScalabriniVilla.com

860 North Quidnessett Road

Phone: (401) 884-1802

N. Kingstown, RI 02852

Fax: (401) 884-4727

Scalabrini Villa is a 120-bed long-term health care facility on 100 acres of scenic land overlooking Narragansett Bay. Scalabrini Villa is a state of the art facility that accommodate long- and short-term care, rehabilitation, respite care, Alzheimer and hospice services. R

Scallop Shell Nursing Home

981 Kingstown Road

Phone: (401) 789-3006

Wakefield, RI 02879

Fax: (401) 789-3562

R

South Bay Manor

www.HorizonBay.com

1959 Kingstown Road

Phone: (401) 789-4880

S. Kingstown, RI 02879

Fax: (401) 792-3780

South County Nursing & Rehab Center   *www.cplsouthcounty.com*

740 Oak Hill Road

N. Kingstown, RI 02852

Phone: (401) 294-4545

Fax: (401) 295-7650

South Kingstown Nursing and Rehab Center   www.hcltdri.com

2115 South County Trail

West Kingston, RI 02892

Phone: (401) 783-8568

Fax: (401) 792-8930

R

Watch Hill Care & Rehab

79 Watch Hill Road

Westerly, RI 02891

Phone: (401) 596-2664

Fax: (401) 596-3666

R

Westerly Health Center

280 High Street

Westerly, RI 02891

Phone: (401) 348-0020

Fax: (401) 596-9783

Westerly Nursing Home

79 Beach Street

Westerly, RI 02891

Phone: (401) 596-4925

Fax: (401) 596-2967

Senior Transition

Services for elders and their families

Toll-Free: (401) 828-5020

—Insured and Bonded-Serving elders and their families

in Rhode Island since 2000—

Email Pat at: sentrans1@verizon.net

www.SeniorTransitionLLC.com

Pat Cusson's Senior Transition helps seniors arrange and handle the mechanics of moving. Pat will arrange for shipping, will negotiate with movers, seek out assisted living options - drawing up floor plans, price comparisons, listing of amenities. She will tackle 45 years of accumulations - encouraging clients to give items to their children, to donate others, to save truly important pieces. She will contact auctioneers and consignment shops. She will arrange for furniture to be delivered (and placed) in the new assisted living apartment. For people new to a community, she will draw up a checklist, offering information on car registration, voter registration, cable television, health insurance. She will fill out the Post Office change-of-address forms. For clients ill-at-ease with computers, she will lead them through the basics of e-mail. Senior Transitions gently guides clients "one step at a time" through the cleaning-up phase and helps adult children work through their mixture of concern and guilt.

Pat left Kent Hospital as the head medical-surgical nurse to start Senior Transition. Her business is one of 200-plus members of a three-year-old nonprofit professional umbrella organization, National Association of Senior Move Managers, comprised of social workers, nurses, decorators and realtors. Senior Transitions is the only Rhode Island member.

2143 Hartford Avenue

Johnston, RI 02919

Phone: (401) 764-0646

Fax: (401) 764-0937

www.seniorsonthemove.com

Seniors on the Move has a keen attention to detail. Whether you are transitioning to or from an assisted living community, or relocating to a different unit, they can manage your move.

Their Elder Liaison will work with you from your initial phone call through your post-move. Their Elder Liaison has years of experience dealing with move-in assistance, space planning, furniture selection with placement and packing/unpacking as needed.

Their dedicated Elder Liaison will take the time go over every aspect of your transition to guarantee that you are comfortable in all phases of your relocation.

Services included from Seniors on the Move range from pre-packing assistance, packing, sorting, and unpacking belongings.

Contact Seniors on the Move's Elder Liaisons, to learn more about their Senior Moving Services.

ELDER ABUSE

FACT:

- In 2003, two of every three elder-abuse victims were women and 43.7% were age 80 or older.

- A 2004 study found that 89.3% of elder abuse takes place in a domestic setting.

- Only 1 in 14 incidents of elder physical abuse that occurs in domestic settings is ever reported to the police.

- Types of elder maltreatment substantiated, include self neglect (37.2%), caregiver neglect (20.4%), emotional, psychological or verbal abuse (14.8%), financial exploitation (14.7%), physical abuse (10.7%), and sexual abuse (1%).

- Only 1 in 25 cases of elder financial exploitation is ever reported.

- Three of every four perpetrators of elder abuse and neglect are under 60 years of age.

- Most alleged offenders are adult children (32.6%) or other family members (21.5%). Spouses or other intimate partners account for 11.3% of the total.

NURSING HOME ABUSE, NEGLECT AND MISTREATMENT: WHAT TO LOOK FOR

Written by Jeffrey M. Padwa, Attorney at Law

Nursing Home Abuse

Bedsores, broken bones, malnutrition, dehydration, and other injuries suffered in nursing homes may be signs of abuse, neglect or mistreatment. Those signs may include unexplained bruises, cuts, burns, sprains, or fractures in various stages of healing; unexplained venereal disease or genital infections; and staff refusing to allow visitors to see a resident, or delays in allowing visitors to see the resident.

Nursing Home Neglect

Nursing home neglect is a general term that covers many different kinds of injuries. Falls, bedsores, elopement, dehydration, malnutrition, and choking on food are all signs of resident neglect.

Bedsores

The areas of the body at greatest risk for developing bedsores are the coccyx, hips, heels, and elbows. The most common cause is when an immobile nursing home resident is not repositioned or turned on a regular basis.

Side Rails and Bed Injuries

Side rails extend either the full length of the bed or part way. Most can be raised or lowered. Side rails are divided with slats spaced about six or more inches apart. This space can trap an elderly person's head, causing him or her to strangle. Often mattresses fit loosely in the frame, leaving gaps large enough to trap the resident between the mattress and side rail, also leading to suffocation and death.

Falls and Fractures

Falls are the most frequent cause of bone fractures among the elderly. Fractures can lead to serious health conditions, such as a difficulty in clearing the chest by coughing (which can lead to pneumonia), a loss of appetite, bedsores, and infections. 25% of elderly who sustain a hip fracture die within 6 months of the injury.

Dehydration

Since elderly persons often have a reduced sense of thirst, dehydration is one of the most frequent causes of hospitalization after age 65. Elderly dehydration is a serious health condition which can lead to death.

Malnutrition

Malnutrition, like dehydration, is a serious health problem among the elderly. Since the elderly have a reduced sense of taste and appetite, proactive steps may be required to prevent physical decline and wrongful death due to starvation.

Wandering/Elopement

Wandering by an elderly person with dementia or Alzheimer's can be a life-threatening situation. The elderly may wander into unsafe areas and be injured or killed. The most dangerous form of wandering is elopement in which the confused person leaves the protected area of the nursing home or assisted living residence and does not return.

Medication Errors

According to an article in the Boston Globe, nearly one out of every 10 nursing home residents suffers a medication-related injury each month. The risk of medication errors is much higher in nursing homes and assisted living residences than in hospital settings due to chronic understaffing.

Choking and Suffocation

Many nursing homes fail to assist or monitor residents, and the tragic result is a high number of deaths due to choking and suffocation. Much like children, many elderly persons who suffer from dementia or Alzheimer's need assistance with eating so they do not put too much food in their mouth at once. Other deaths can be caused by strangulation from restraints.

Physical and Sexual Assault

Sexual assault statistics indicate the widespread problem of rape and sexual assaults in nursing homes and assisted living residences. In legal terms, sexual assault includes any forced sexual contact that can range from unwanted touching to sexual penetration. The impact left because of sexual assault can be physically, psychologically and emotionally damaging.

**If you are concerned about a family member's care in a nursing home, assisted living residence or other extended care facility contact an attorney with experience in these cases.

DEPARTMENT OF ELDERLY AFFAIRS PROTECTIVE SERVICES

Phone: (401) 462-0555

The DEA Protective Services Unit is responsible for investigating complaints of elderly abuse of Rhode Islanders 60 years of age and older by a family member, caregiver or person with duty of care. Abuse may include physical, emotional, sexual, financial exploitation, or abandonment.

Rhode Island law requires any person who has reasonable cause to believe that an elderly person has been abused to report it to DEA. Failure to report abuse of a person 60 years of age or older can result in a fine of up to $1,000.

The DEA Protective Services Unit develops a care plan to prevent additional abuse and address the elder's social service needs.

Self-Neglect occurs when a person is no longer able to care for himself/herself. Reports of self-neglect are also made to the DEA Protective Services Unit. The senior's needs are assessed and necessary services are offered.

Under Rhode Island law, DEA records pertaining to a person reported to be abused, neglected, exploited or abandoned are confidential and are not deemed public records.

To file an elderly abuse or self-neglect report, call the Department of Elderly Affairs Protective Services Unit at (401) 462-0555.

ELIZABETH BUFFUM CHACE CENTER

Post Office Box 9476

Warwick, Rhode Island 02889

Business Phone: (401) 738-9700

24 Hour Crisis Hotline: (401) 738-1700

Fax: (401) 738-1713

Advocacy, support and protection for victims of domestic violence.

Confidential

- Staffed 24 hours a day by advocated trained to provide information, referrals, support, and individual safety plans for women or men victimized in a relationship.

- Short-term safe, confidential shelter for women and children in danger.

- No caller Identification

- All phone lines are blocked to ensure confidentiality

- Counseling and Support Groups

- Assistance at Police Departments

- Court advocates available to assist victims of domestic violence

ALL SUPPORT SERVICES ARE FREE OF CHARGE

NO ONE DESRVES ABUSE.

HELP IS AVAILABLE.

OTHER DOMESTIC VIOLENCE RESOURCES

Rhode Island Coalition Against Domestic Violence

www.ricadv.org

24 Hour Hotline: 1-800-494-8100

Telephone: (401) 467-9940

The Rhode Island Coalition Against Domestic Violence works to eliminate domestic violence in Rhode Island. Its mission is to support and enhance the work of its member agencies and to provide leadership on the issue of domestic violence. The Coalition has a 24 Hour hotline. Additionally, the Coalition has published a **"Guide to Living Safely for Older Adults"**. Call 401-467-9940 to obtain a Guide.

Senior Citizen Police Advocates are police officers that are designated to make changes on the behalf of senior citizens regarding state legislature, specifically in cases of abuse and in dealing with elderly violators.

Town	Advocate	Telephone
Barrington	Josh Birrell/ Joseph Benedetti	437-3930
Block Island	Vincent Carlone	466-3220
Bristol	Adam Clifford	253-6900
Burrillville	Brian Pitts	568-6255
Central Falls	Max Gonzales	727-7411
Charlestown	Jack Shippee	364-1212
Coventry	David Fraatz	826-1100
Cranston	Carl Ricci	477-5073
Cumberland	Michael Kinch	333-2500
East Greenwich	John Carter	884-2244
East Providence	Thomas Aguia	435-7630
Exeter	William Jamieson	444-1068
Foster	William Ziehl	397-3317
Glocester	Kimberly Bertholic /Alan Gusdafson	568-2533
Hopkinton	John Patton	377-7750
Jamestown	John Dube	423-1212
Johnston	James Amodei	231-4210
Lincoln	Brian Sullivan	333-1111
Little Compton	Sue Cressman	635-2311
Middletown	Fred Bodington	846-1144
Narragansett	Anthony Pelopida, Jr.	789-1091
North Kingstown	Daniel Ormond	294-3316
Newport	Jimmy Winters	847-1302
North Providence	Joseph Sanita/ John Anzivino	233-1433
North Smithfield	Sharon Pagliarini	762-1212

Town	Advocate	Telephone
Pawtucket	Angelo Squadrito	727-9100
Portsmouth	Brett Bucholz	683-0300
Providence	William Merandi	243-6407
Richmond	Raymond Driscoll	539-8289
Scituate	Donald Delaere	821-5900
Smithfield	Orlando Braxton/ Robert Squillante	231-2500
South Kingstown	Paul Horoho	783-3321
Tiverton	Ken Cabral	625-6716
Warren	Ray Verges	245-1311
Warwick	Steve Lombardi	468-4325
Westerly	Unavailable	596-2022
West Greenwich	Ray Cappelli	397-7191
West Warwick	Sandra Marinucci	821-4323
Woonsocket	John Donlon	766-1212
State Police	Joseph Meich	444-1000

Notes

HOSPITALS

Bradley Hospital

1011 Veterans Memorial Parkway

East Providence, RI 02915

Phone: (401) 432-1000

www.LifeSpan.org/Bradley

Butler Hospital

345 Blackstone Boulevard

Providence, RI 02906

Phone: (401) 455-6200

www.Butler.org

Eleanor Slater Hospital

14 Harrington Road

Cranston, RI 02920

Phone: (401) 462-2319

www.MHRH.RI.gov/ESH

Hasbro Children's Hospital

593 Eddy Street

Providence, RI 02903

Phone: 401-444-4000

www.LifeSpan.org/HCH

Kent Hospital

455 Toll Gate Road

Warwick, Rhode Island 02886

Phone: (401) 737-7000

wwww.KentHospital.org

Landmark Medical Center

115 Cass Avenue

Woonsocket, RI

Phone: (401) 769-4100

www.LandmarkMedical.org

Memorial Hospital of RI

111 Brewster Street

Pawtucket, RI 02860

Phone: (401) 729-2000

www.MHRIweb.org

The Miriam Hospital

164 Summit Avenue   Phone: (401) 793-2500

Providence, RI 02906   *www.LifeSpan.org / TMH*

Newport Hospital

11 Friendship Street   Phone: (401) 846-6400

Newport, RI 02840   *www.LifeSpan.org / Newport*

Our Lady of Fatima Hospital

200 High Service Avenue   Phone: (401) 456-3000

N. Providence, RI 0290   *www.FatimaHospital.com*

Rehabilitation Hospital of RI

116 Eddie Dowling Highway   Phone: (401) 766-0800

N. Smithfield, RI 02896   *www.RHRI.net*

Rhode Island Hospital

593 Eddy Street   Phone: (401) 444-4000

Providence, RI 02903   *www.LifeSpan.org / RIH*

Roger Williams Medical Center

825 Chalkstone Avenue   Phone: (401) 456-2000

Providence, RI 02908   *www.RWMC.org*

South County Hospital

100 Kenyon Avenue   Phone: (401) 782-8000

Wakefield, RI 0287   *www.SCHospital.com*

St. Joseph Hospital for Specialty Care

21 Peace Street

Providence, RI 02904

Phone: (401) 456-3000

www.SpecialtyCareRI.com

The Westerly Hospital

25 Wells Street

Westerly, RI 02891

Phone: (401) 596-6000

www.WesterlyHospital.org

Women & Infants Hospital

101 Dudley Street

Providence, Rhode Island 02905

Phone: (401) 274-1100

www.WomenAndInfants.org

Notes

Notes

HOSPICE CARE
PROVIDERS

Beacon Hospice, Inc.

www.BeaconHospice.com

1 Catamore Boulevard

Phone: (401) 438-0008

East Providence, RI 02914

Fax: (401) 438-2252

Alternate Location

6946 Post Road

Phone: (401) 884-3845

North Kingstown, RI 02852

Fax: (401) 884-3848

Home & Hospice Care of Rhode Island

Main Office

1085 North Main Street

Phone: (401) 727-7070

Providence, RI 02904

Toll Free: (800) 338-6555

South Office

143 Main Street

Phone: (401) 789-5200

Wakefield, RI 02879

Toll Free: (800) 228-4230

Philip Hulitar Center Inpatient Facility

www.HHCRI.net

50 Maude Street

Phone: (401) 351-5570

Providence, RI 02908

Toll Free: (877) 322-1678

*Patients at Aquidneck Island may call (800) 228-4230.

Hospice at VNS of Newport & Bristol Counties *www.VNSRI.com*

1184 East Main Road

Phone: (401) 847-2201

Portsmouth, RI 02871

Fax: (401) 682-2111

Odyssey HealthCare of Rhode Island

2374 Post Road, Suite 206

Warwick, RI 02886

www.OdsyHealth.com

Phone: (401) 738-1492

Fax: (401) 738-4029

VNA of Care New England

51 Health Lane

Warwick, RI 02886

www.VNACNE.com

Phone: (401) 737-6050

Fax: (401) 732-6210

VNA of Rhode Island Hospice

475 Kilvert Street

Warwick, RI 02886

www.VNARI.org

Phone: (401) 574-4900

Fax: (401) 490-8870

Please fax referrals or call intake directly at 401-574-4950.

VNS of Greater Rhode Island

6 Blackstone Valley Place, Suite 515

Lincoln, RI 02865

www.VNSGRI.org

Phone: (401) 769-5670

Fax: (401) 762-2966

VNA of Southeastern Massachusetts

115 East Main Road

Little Compton, RI 02837

www.VNASM.org

Phone: (401) 635-2358

Fax: (401) 635-1694

Notes

SENIOR DRIVING
&
DEMENTIA

SENIOR DRIVING ISSUES & CONCERNS

It is often difficult for aging individuals to recognize their changing abilities. Most seniors believe they will know when it is time to stop driving. For most people, driving is a sign of independence, control, competence and social responsibility. Consequently, giving up the keys can be devastating to seniors who view it as a loss of independence and self-sufficiency. The following article offers tips for seniors and others for recognizing unsafe driving, and guidance on handling decisions about driving.

First, it is important for seniors to know the signs of decreasing driving skills and adjust their driving habits to compensate for the decrease. For example, a senior who recognizes a decrease in driving skills could restrict his or her driving to:

- Daylight hours
- Off-peak traffic hours
- Familiar roads
- Shorter trips
- Lower speed roads

The AARP has published a "Close Call Quiz" as part of its Driver Safety Program to help drivers recognize diminishing driving skills. The AARP states that a "yes" answer to any of the ten questions may indicate that the driver perhaps had a close call for an accident. The ten questions are as follows:

1. Do you sometimes say, "Whew, that was close!"

2. At times, do cars seem to appear from nowhere?

3. At intersections, do cars sometimes proceed when you felt you had the right of way?

4. Are gaps in traffic harder to judge?

5. Do others honk at you?

6. After driving, do you feel physically exhausted?

7. Do you think you are slower than you used to be in reacting to dangerous driving situations?

8. Have you had an increased number of near accidents in the past year?

9. Do you find it difficult to decide when to join traffic on a busy interstate highway?

10. Do intersections bother you because there is so much to watch for in all directions?

Family, friends, physicians, care-managers and other individuals close to a senior are pivotal in identifying a senior's functional limitations that may impair driving performance and lead to unsafe decisions. Some physical signs that driving may be dangerous are loss of hearing, vision problems, health problems like arthritis, sleepiness, attention problems, and other medical conditions which may affect driving skills, such as dementia. Driving behavior that may indicate a person's driving threatens personal safety and that of others includes:

- Has difficulty following instructions

- Drifts into other lanes of traffic

- Stops abruptly without cause

- Presses simultaneously on the brake and accelerator while driving

- Delays changing lanes when an obstacle appears in the lane which he or she is driving.

- Does not use turn signals

- Straddles lanes

- Does not react to emergency situations

- Is increasingly nervous when driving

- Has difficulty seeing

Dealing with older family members diagnosed with dementia or Alzheimer's disease means family members need to take a more active role in making driving decisions. Since memory loss is associated with these diseases, the person often does not remember that he or she cannot drive. Explaining to the person can often lead to frustration and arguments. The Alzheimer's Association makes the following recommendations to family members:

- Begin with early planning. Have the person diagnosed with dementia sign an agreement with his/her family about driving. The Agreement can state who is allowed to make a decision to take away the keys, making that difficult decision that driving is no longer safe. Anyone can draft this simple Agreement for you and, while it may not be enforceable, it allows the senior to be an active participant in his/her future planning and decision making. Dignity cannot be overlooked.

- Get a prescription from the doctor that states "No driving".

- Have a physician order a driving evaluation. There is a list of driving evaluation resources in Rhode Island included in this section.

- Distract the family member who insists on driving, diverting his or her attention to something else.

- Control access to car keys by keeping them out of view, bending the keys, or filing them down. This should be a last resort.

- Disable the car by removing the distributor cap or unplugging the starter wire. This should be a last resort.

- Move the car out of sight.

- Sell the car and blame financial reasons for doing so, such as registration, insurance, gasoline, and regular maintenance costs.

Seek other sources of support, such as from your lawyer, geriatric care manager, and the Alzheimer's Association—RI Chapter. Most importantly, support from friends and family members is crucial to helping the senior through this time in his or her life.

Independent On-Road Evaluator

Phone: (860) 208-9540

Contact: Tim Souza

Procedure: The driver of concern can be self-referred or can be referred by a physician. A generalized road test that focuses on the evaluation o skills needed to drive safely. The road test can take up to two hours.

The report is prepared and given to the driver of concern and their family or friend. A report is also sent to the referring physician.

Cost: Approximately $150

Registry of Motor Vehicles-Operator Control Division

30 Howard Avenue, Building 58

Cranston, RI 02920

Phone: (401) 721-2650

Procedure: Anybody, including the physician, can send a letter to the Operator Control Division containing a short description of the driving concerns and incidents observed. The identity of the person who contacts the Division is kept confidential. When the letter is received, the driver of concern is asked to come into the office for a hearing. At the hearing, it is determined whether or not a road test or further evaluation is needed. After the evaluation, a decision will be made regarding the status of the driver's license, including possible suspension or revocation.

Cost: Free

Rhode Island Department of Rehabilitative Medicine

Phone: (401) 444-5418

Contact: Laura Richard

Procedure: The driver of concern can be self-referred or can be referred by a physician. After an in-office clinical assessment is performed, there may be a road test. The report is prepared and given to the driver of concern and their family or friend. A report is also sent to the referring physician.

Cost: Insurance may pay for in-office clinical assessment. The on road evaluation is $150.

South County Hospital Outpatient Occupational Therapy

Phone: (401) 789-2044

Contact: Linda Curry

Procedure: The driver of concern can be self-referred or can be referred by a physician. After an in-office clinical assessment is performed, there may be a road test. The report is prepared and given to the driver of concern and their family or friend. A report is also sent to the referring physician.

Cost: Insurance may pay for in-office clinical assessment. The on road evaluation is $125

Notes

TRANSPORTATION PROGRAMS

THE RIDE PROGRAM

333 Melrose Street

Providence, RI 02907

Phone: (401) 461-9760

(800) 479-6902

www.RIPTA.com

The RIde program provides transportation for individuals with disabilities and seniors. It is based on the eligibility requirements of several state agency programs.

The Department of Elderly Affairs, The Department of Human Services, Rhode Island Public Transit Authority, and a group of ARC's of Rhode Island are the major funding agency partners in the RIde Program. Some towns and nonprofit agencies also participate.

Each agency has its own program eligibility rules. RIde coordinates share ride services among all eligible passengers. Call for more detailed information.

RHODE ISLAND PUBLIC TRANSIT AUTHORITY (RIPTA)

265 Melrose Street

Providence, RI 02907

Phone: (401) 784-9500

www.RIPTA.com

Rhode Islanders of any age who have a disability may be eligible for Americans with Disabilities Act (ADA) Paratransit Services from the Rhode Island Public Transit Authority (RIPTA) curb-to-curb transportation service to people with disabilities which prevent them from using regular RIPTA bus service. This service is provided along existing RIPTA service corridors at a cost of twice the standard bus rate for all riders. To apply, call (401) 784-9500.

RIPTA bus passes cost residents aged 65 or older $5 and are valid for 5 years. Qualified riders who have a disability pay $2 for their 2-year pass. Pass holders pay half-fare on off-peak hours, weekends, and holidays. Bus pass holders enrolled in Medical Assistance (Medicaid) or RIPAE Level One income guidelines may apply for the No Fare program and ride free during all hours. Call RIPTA at 784-9500 *604 for details and/or more information.

These communities provide additional transportation for their senior residents:

City/Town:	Phone:
Barrington	(401) 247-1926
Bristol	(401) 253-8458
Burrillville	(401) 568-4440
Coventry	(401) 822-9175
Cranston	(401) 943-3341
Lincoln	(401) 723-3270
Narragansett	(401) 782-0675
North Kingstown	(401) 268-1590
North Providence	(401) 231-0749
North Smithfield	(401) 765-3535
Pawtucket	(401) 725-8220
Scituate	(401) 647-2662
Smithfield	(401) 949-4592
South Kingstown	(401) 789-0268
Warren	(401) 245-8140
Warwick	(401) 738-1276
Woonsocket	(401) 766-3734

Notes

SENIOR IDENTIFICATION CARDS

SENIOR IDENTIFICATION CARDS

The Rhode Island Division of Motor Vehicles issues photo identification cards to Rhode Island residents age 59 and older and adults with disabilities. You must have proof of residence, proof of age, proof of signature, and proof of disability if under the age of 59. There is no fee.

The following Department of Motor Vehicle sites offer Senior Identification Cards:

Middletown DMV

73 Valley Road, Middletown,RI

Open Monday through Friday, 8:30am—3:30pm.

Pawtucket DMV

100 Main Street, Pawtucket, RI

Open Monday through Friday, 8:30am—3:15pm.

Wakefield

Stedman Government Center, Tower Hill Road, Wakefield, RI

Open Wednesday and Thursday, 8:30am-3:30pm.

Warren DMV

1 Joyce Street, Warren, RI

Open Tuesdays from 8:30am –3:30pm.

Woonsocket DMV

217 Pond Street, Department of Labor Bldg., Woonsocket, RI

Open: Tuesday through Friday, 8:30am –3:30pm.

MEAL ASSISTANCE PROGRAMS

THE OCEAN STATE SENIOR DINING PROGRAM:

The Ocean State Dining Program provides nutritionally balanced, hot lunches served five days a week at more than 75 meal sites for persons who are 60 years of age or older or disabled. In the case of a married couple, one person must be 60 years of age or older.

Seniors may donate to the cost of the meal, but no one is refused a meal if unable to contribute. Transportation to the nearest meal site is available. At least 24 hours notice is required for reservations.

To locate your local meal site, please call:

Locations:	Phone:
Northwest RI (C.O.A.S.I)	(401) 728-9290
East Bay, Bristol & Newport (East Bay CAP)	(401) 437-1000
Kent and Washington (West Bay CAP)	(401) 732-5660
Northern RI (Woonsocket Sr. Svcs.)	(401) 766-3734
Providence (Meals on Wheels)	(401) 351-6700

BLACKSTONE HEALTH INC. NUTRITION PROGRAM

420 Main Street

Pawtucket, RI 02860

Phone: (401) 728-9290

www.blackstonehealth.org

With 15 meal sites within the state of Rhode Island, Blackstone Health Inc. Nutrition Program operates congregate meal sites in Pawtucket, Central Falls, North Providence, Johnston, Coventry, Cranston, North Kingstown, Providence, and Scituate. Participants are able to enjoy a nutritious meal along with good company, and nutritional education through the use of newsletters, seminars, and individual dietary counseling, as needed.

The program is personalized to meet the nutritional needs of its elderly population and strives to help seniors become more independent in a friendly and welcoming setting. The program aims to assist many seniors who otherwise may be isolated within their homes.

Blackstone Health Inc. provides 200,000 meals annually and offers nutrition counseling to improve the independence of each participant. The Nutrition Program utilizes senior employees; however, volunteers are heavily relied on and always welcome.

For more information, please contact the Nutrition Director at 401-728-9290 or the Nutrition Assistant at 401-365-1101.

70 Bath Street

Providence, RI 02908

Phone: (401) 351-6700

www.rimeals.org

For over 40 years, Meals on Wheels of Rhode Island has provided home delivered and congregate meals to Rhode Island seniors. Providing necessary nutrition, the meals contribute to continuing independence for many seniors; keeping them in their homes rather than in an institutional setting. *There is no charge* for home delivered or congregate meals, however a $3.00 donation per meal is suggested.

The Meals on Wheels of Rhode Island Home Delivered Meal Program services almost 4,000 individuals annually. To be eligible to receive meals one must have an inability to cook due to a physical/psychological impairment, live alone (with no help preparing meals), be 60 years of age or older (or on the DEA or DHS waiver program), have no help preparing meals, and be unable to drive or attend a congregate meal site.

For Providence area seniors who are able to leave their homes, the *Congregate Meal Program* provides a delicious hot meal in a community setting. Congregate meals keep seniors engaged in a social environment, while also offering nutritional workshops, newsletters, and more. There are three Providence locations and diners "pay" using a voucher.

For information on receiving meals, obtaining vouchers, or volunteering for Meals on Wheels programs, please call (401) 351-6700.

The Rhode Island Community Food Bank

200 Niantic Avenue

Providence, RI 02905

(401) 942-6325

www.rifoodbank.org

✳

The Poverello Center

668 Hartford Avenue

Providence, RI 02909

(401) 455-3740

✳

The Rhode Island Coalition for the Homeless

160 Broad Street

Providence, RI 02909

(401) 421-6458

✳

Crossroads Rhode Island

160 Broad Street

Providence, RI 02909

(401) 521-2255

✳

Comprehensive Community Action Program

311 Doric Avenue

Cranston, RI 02921

(401) 467-9610

FOOD STAMP PROGRAM

The food stamp program helps low-income households purchase food. Possible deductions from gross income may include a standard deduction for household and telephone expenses, an earned income deduction for working households and specified deductions for medical expenses and excess shelter costs. Adults who are eligible for the Food Stamp program receive their benefits using a special Electronic Benefit Transfer (EBT) card. Individuals can use their EBT card at grocery and retail food stores across the state.

For more information regarding the Food Stamp program or to request a home interview, please call the following offices:

Newport/Aquidneck Island	(401) 849-6000
Northern Rhode Island	(401) 235-6300
Pawtucket	(401) 729-5400
Providence	(401) 222-7276
South County	(800) 282-7021

Notes

PRESCRIPTION
ASSISTANCE
PROGRAMS

RIPAE

The Rhode Island Pharmaceutical Assistance to the Elderly (RIPAE) program pays a portion of the cost of Category A prescriptions used to treat the following:

- Alzheimer's disease
- Arthritis
- Diabetes
- Heart Problems
- Depression
- Circulatory insufficiency
- High cholesterol
- Asthma
- Mineral supplements

- Anti-infectives
- Parkinson's disease
- High blood pressure
- Cancer
- Urinary inconsistence
- Chronic respiratory conditions
- Osteoporosis
- Glaucoma
- Prescriptions vitamins

RIPAE also offer limited coverage for the cost of injectable prescription drugs used to treat Multiple Sclerosis.

RIPAE enrollees can purchase all other FDA-approved Category B prescriptions (except for those used to treat cosmetic conditions) at the RIPAE discounted price. Additionally, no state co-pay is needed for medications in this category.

Also under RIPAE, Rhode Island residents between 55 and 64 who are receiving Social Security Disability Income payments and who meet specified income limits, can purchase medications (except those prescribed for cosmetic conditions) at a discounted price.

For more specific questions regarding ones annual income and program eligibility please contact RIPAE at (401) 462-4000.

PHARMACEUTICAL RESEARCH AND MANUFACTURERS OF AMERICA

Many pharmaceutical manufacturers yield some of their drugs available free of charge to patients who have trouble paying for them. These voluntary programs, where each manufacturer creates its own eligibility criteria, typically require a physician to make direct contact with the selected manufacturer. Available drugs are generally used to treat long term illnesses.

For more information please contact the Pharmaceutical Research and Manufacturers of America at **(877) 743-6779** or visit *www.rxforri.com*.

UNIVERSITY OF RHODE ISLAND (URI) PHARMACY OUTREACH PROGRAM

This program assists Rhode Island residents regarding the availability of free or low cost medications through the Medication for the Needy Program. The program also provides educational seminars, health screens, and discussion groups on health related topics. Pharmacist are readily available to answer medication questions.

For more information please contact the University of Rhode Island (URI) Pharmacy Outreach Program at **(800) 215-9001** or visit *www.uri.edu/pharmacy/outreach*.

Notes

VETERANS SERVICES
& RESOURCES

Middletown VA Community Based Outpatient Clinic

One Corporate Place

West Main & Northgate

Middletown, RI 02842

Phone: (401) 847-6239

Fax: (401) 847-8057

The Middletown VA facility provides comprehensive health care to veterans residing in Newport, Bristol, and Washington Counties. Every patient has a primary care provider who coordinates his or her health care needs. You can contact the Clinic for information on how to enroll or to arrange for a tour.

The Cremation Society of Rhode Island

571 W. Greenville Road, P.O. Box 216

North Scituate, RI 02857

Phone: (401) 647-0620

Toll Free: (800) 941-2211 (Available 24 Hours a Day)

www.csori.com

Under certain circumstances, the Veterans Administration provides cash benefits for reimbursement of burial expenses, a burial plot allowance, transportation allowance, a United States flag, Headstone or Marker, and free Grave Space.

The Providence Regional Office of the
Veterans Benefits Administration

380 Westminster Street

Providence, RI 02903

Phone: (800) 827-1000

www.va.gov

The Providence Regional Office is responsible for the management
of most non-medial benefits provided by the Veterans
Administration, including compensation, pension, vocational
rehabilitation and counseling.

The Providence VA Medical Center

830 Chalkstone Boulevard

Providence, RI 02908

Toll Free: (866) 590-2976

Fax: (401) 457-3370

www.providence.va.gov/about

The Providence VA Medical Center provides outpatient and
inpatient healthcare to veterans residing in Rhode Island and
southeastern Massachusetts. A Primary Care Provider coordinates
each patient's medical care, patient education needs and referrals to
any of the medical centers 32 subspecialty clinics. The Medical
Center's Ambulatory Care Program is supported by a general
medical, surgical, and psychiatric inpatient facility fully-accredited
by the Joint Commission on the Accreditation of Healthcare
Organizations (JCAHO). The medical center delivers a broad range
of services in medicine, surgery, and behavioral sciences and is
currently operating 73 beds.

The Rhode Island Veterans Affairs Office

480 Metacom Avenue

Bristol, RI 02809

Phone: (401) 253-8000 *695

Fax: (401)254-2320

www.dhs.state.ri.us

The Rhode Island Veterans Affairs Office offers Veterans benefit counseling including a the processing of all applications for admissions to the RI Veterans Home in Bristol, casework, counseling, referral and claims relating to pensions, compensations and Social Security. The Office also offers social services to Rhode Island armed forces personnel, veterans, and their dependents who are seeking assistance.

The Rhode Island Veterans Cemetery

301 South County Trail

Exeter, RI 02822

Phone: (401) 268-3088

www.dhs.state.ri.us

The Rhode Island Veterans Cemetery is comprised of 265 acres of land in Exeter, providing a final resting place for honorably discharged Rhode Island Veterans who have served during wartime, and their dependents. Eligibility requirements: the Veteran must have been discharged with "Honorable Service," have entered into the service from Rhode Island or have lived in Rhode Island two years prior to death, have had active duty during wartime, two or more consecutive years of active duty during peacetime, or have twenty years of National Guard Reserve time.

The Rhode Island Veterans Home

480 Metacom Avenue

Bristol, RI 02809

Phone: (401) 253-8000 *695

The Rhode Island Veterans Home is a 110 Acre complex located on Mount Hope Bay. The mission of the Home is to provide quality nursing and residential care to eligible Rhode Island Veterans and their dependents and/or survivors to improve their physical, emotional, and economic well-being

The Home has 260 nursing care beds in three skilled and semi-skilled units and two ambulatory care units with an additional 79 beds.

Eligibility requirements: the Veteran must have been discharged with "Honorable Service", have entered into the service from Rhode Island or have lived in Rhode Island two years prior to death, and have had acquired a service-related disability or disease.

Notes

SENIOR ADVOCACY GROUPS & CONSUMER PROTECTION

CONSUMER PROTECTION

The Better Business Bureau

The Better Business Bureau tracks information on business in Rhode Island and other states. If you have a complaint against a business, or wish to inquire about a business prior to engaging services, call 1-800-422-2811 for more information, or visit www.rhodeisland.bbb.org.

National Do Not Call Registry

This Registry allows individuals to limit the number of phone call received by telemarketers. For more information, call 1-888-382-1222, or visit www.donotcall.gov.

Attorney General's Consumer Protection Unit

The Rhode Island Consumer Protection Unit handles complaints against Rhode Island businesses. If you feel as though you have been victimized by a scam, fraud, or scheme, you should call and you should also contact your local police department. For more information, call 401-274-4400.

LEGAL SERVICES

Rhode Island Disability Law Center

275 Westminster Street, Suite 401   www.ridlc.org

Providence, RI 02901   Phone: 401) 831-3150

TTY (401) 831-5335

The Rhode Island Disability Law Center provides free legal assistance to disabled residents. Services include individual legal representation to protect rights or to secure benefits and services, self-help information, educational programs and administrative and legislative advocacy.

Rhode Island Legal Services Senior Citizens Program

56 Pine Street   Phone: (401) 274-2652

Providence, RI 02903   1-800-662-5034

TTY: 401-272-5335

The Rhode Island Legal Services Senior Citizens Program *helps low income persons age 60 and older* with legal advice and assistance for housing, Social Security, Medicaid, Medicare, and Food Stamp matters.

Laura M. Krohn, Elder Law Attorney, Inc. & Senior Resource Clinic

631 Main Street   www.seniorguideri.com

East Greenwich, RI 02818   Phone: (401) 398-8383

Offering legal services including Wills, Trusts, Powers of Attorney, Living Wills, Guardianship, Asset Protection, Medicaid, Special Needs Planning,, and Estate Administration. Call for consultation with Laura.

For those unsure of their needs, the Senior Clinic is open Monday – Friday, 9:00-5:00pm. Stop by and gather free resources and literature that will help you begin your journey through senior services in RI.

The Rhode Island Advisory Commission on Aging

(401) 462-0509

The commission was created in 1977 and advises the Governor and the Director of the Department of Elderly Affairs regarding issues and problems confronting elders and adults with disabilities.

❋

The Rhode Island Forum on Aging

(401) 462-0509

The Forum was established in 1991 and provides a focal point on aging issues, provides information on these issues, and establishes priorities for advocacy.

❋

The Rhode Island Long Term Care Coordinating Council

(401) 222-2371

The Council was created in 1987 and is committed to bringing quality, affordable and accessible long term care to Rhode Islanders.

❋

Senior Action in a Gay Environment

(401) 751-1487

SAGE offers support and social opportunities to elder gay persons.

❋

The Silver Haired Legislature

(401) 462-0509

www.RISHL.org

The Legislature was created in 1981 and is composed of senior representing each legislative district in Rhode Island. Efforts are focused on advocating for senior issues by promoting knowledge of the governmental and legislative process.

The AARP

1-866-542-8170

10 Orms Street, Providence, RI 0296

AARP-Rhode Island is a non-profit, non-partisan organization for those 50 and older. AARP lobbies federal and state government for programs and services that enhance the quality of life for seniors.

www.aarp.org/ri

The Point

401-462-4444

171 Service Road, Warwick, RI 02886

Call the point for information regarding how you can access any of the groups listed here, or other groups, that will allow you as a senior to influence public policy.

www.ThePointRI.org

The Gray Panthers of Rhode Island

401-274-6900

133 Mathewson Street, Providence, RI 02903

The Gray Panthers of Rhode Island is part of an intergenerational advocacy organizations that works for social and economic justice.

SENIOR AGENDA COALITION OF RHODE ISLAND

133 Matthewson Street

Providence, RI 02903

Phone: (401) 274-6900

www.SeniorAgendaRI.org

The Senior Agenda Coalition is a diverse coalition of activists and groups that advocate for the elderly organized to develop a common agenda to improve the quality of life of older Rhode Islanders. The coalition empowers people and organizations to discuss issues, promote legislation, and influence policies of both public and private institutions to further the common agenda.

One of the Coalition's greatest strengths is the ability to engage coalition members in their mission and work collaboratively with other organizations. Their intent and core purpose is to create and sustain this collaborative effort.

Campaigns include advocacy at the State House by seniors and advocates, attending all hearings on top priority bills, attending meetings with legislators at the Statehouse and in their districts, petitions, phone calls, and press events. Efforts are focused on monitoring the implementation of laws and working with the State Departments on regulation of programs.

In addition to the valuable research of our Best Practices Reports and Senior Agenda Fact book, they offer Elder Policy Advocate training which helps the Senior Agenda develop a base of trained advocates. These trainings educate seniors and advocates on how policy works, why it is important, and how to share stories.

The Senior Agenda Coalition also holds Senior Issues Candidates' Forums during election years. The Coalition has had great success sponsoring these highly attended events in the past. These forums help the Coalition build relationships with the candidates once they are in office, generate a lot of press, and help to educate and motivate seniors and advocates to push for legislation that benefits the elderly.

Notes

THE ALZHEIMER'S ASSOCIATION
RHODE ISLAND CHAPTER

ABOUT THE RHODE ISLAND CHAPTER
—A LETTER FROM THE EXECUTIVE DIRECTOR—
Donna M. McGowan

alzheimer's association™

"The compassion to care, the leadership to conquer." That describes the work of the Alzheimer's Association.

The Rhode Island Chapter is a private, non-profit organization that provides education, personal support, and advocacy around key issues of concern to those persons in Rhode Island affected by this disease. It is supported solely through contributions from individuals as well as by public and private grants.

The services of the Rhode Island Chapter seek to assist both the 25,000 people in the State who have the disease and their care partners.

- The Early Stage Live and Learn Program utilizes a public library and other community sites to provide meaningful activities and socialization for those in the beginning stages of Alzheimer's disease.

- The agency HELPLINE provides 24 hour access to information and referral. (1-800-272-3900)

- Affiliated statewide support groups and community education presentations reach caregivers throughout Rhode Island.

- Medic Alert and Safe Return, the nationwide identification/ registration system gives more peace of mind when families are faced with wandering of loved ones with Alzheimer's disease.

- A research lecture, every November, informs the statewide community of the status of progress in finding better treatment and ultimately, a cure.

All family services are free of charge.

The RI Chapter offers a wide variety of training geared to health care professionals. Staff at home care agencies, adult day centers, assisted living and nursing facilities learn how to manage the needs of Alzheimer patients. Special Care Units are examined by Chapter staff to provide greater assistance to those who care for people in later stages of the disease.

The Alzheimer's Association website helps both professionals and family members to gain extensive information on all aspects of Alzheimer's. A resource library in the RI Chapter office offers a plethora of valuable resources as well.

The Alzheimer's Association-RI Chapter advocates to improve the long term care health delivery system. As a member of the State Long Term Care Coordinating Council and the Senior Agenda Coalition, the agency works in conjunction with other advocates to bring about improvements.

There are very few people whose lives are not touched by Alzheimer's disease. Because of this wide-ranging impact, the Rhode Island Chapter can always use help. We encourage you to contact us!

Rhode Island Chapter

245 Waterman Street, Suite 306

Providence, RI 02906

(401) 421-0008 or (800) 272-3900

www.alz.org/ri

From Left: Laura M. Krohn, *Elder Law Attorney* and Elizabeth Morancy, *former Executive Director* of the Alzheimer's Association— Rhode Island Chapter, walking to help end Alzheimer's disease

Here are a few ways you can assist the Alzheimer's Association—Rhode Island Chapter.

- **Participate in the Memory Walk**

  Memory Walk is the nation's largest event to raise awareness and funds for Alzheimer's care, support and research. You can be a walker, sponsor a walker, start your own team or volunteer. For more information, go to www.alz.org/memorywalk

- **Volunteer** your experience/expertise for community presentations or help out in the RI Chapter office

- **Make a donation** in memory of a loved one or to honor someone affected by the disease.

- **Purchase Live & Learn Note cards** created by the participation of the Live & Learn Program. Cards are $5.00 for four cards. Proceeds support the Live & Learn Program.

- **Purchase Beaded Bookmarks** created by the participants of the Live & Learn Program. Bookmarks are $5.00 and proceeds support the Live & Learn Program.

- **Purchase a Forget-Me-Not Flower Pin**

  These pins are made in Rhode Island for Rhode Islanders with Alzheimer's disease. The pins cost $20 each. All proceeds from pin sales will directly help Rhode Island families dealing with the challenges of Alzheimer's disease.

THANKS FOR YOUR SUPPORT!

Contact Camilla Farrell, Development Director of the Rhode Island Chapter, for further information about how you can help.

(401) 421-0008 or 1-800-272-3900

MEDICALERT® + SAFE RETURN®

Alzheimer's Association MedicAlert® + Safe Return® is a nationwide identification, support and enrollment program working at the community level. The specially designed service provides assistance whether a person becomes lost locally or far from home. Assistance is available 24 hours, every day, whenever a person is lost or found. The Alzheimer's Association is the trusted resource for information, education , referral, and support millions of people affected by the disease, their families and caregivers.

With a $49.95 enrollment in the Alzheimer's Association MedicAlert® + Safe Return® program, you will receive the following products:

1) Engraved identification bracelet or necklace and iron-on clothing labels

2) Caregiver checklist, key chain, label pin, refrigerator magnet, stickers and wallet cards.

3) For an additional $25, you'll receive caregiver jewelry.
In an emergency, it alerts others that you provide care for a person enrolled in Safe Return®.

If an enrollee is missing, the Alzheimer's Association MedicAlert® + Safe Return® program can fax the person's information and photograph to local law enforcement.

If an enrollee is found, a citizen or law official can call the number on the identification products and MedicAlert® + Safe Return® can access enrollee information and notify listed contacts.

For further information contact the Alzheimer's Association—

Rhode Island Chapter at (401) 421-0008 or visit www.medicalert.org/safereturn

230

You can enroll in MedicAlert® + Safe Return® in
one of the following ways:

Send a completed enrollment form, photograph and payment to:

Alzheimer's Association Medic Alert® + Safe Return®

2323 Colorado Avenue

Turlock, California 95382

OR

Alzheimer's Association—Rhode Island Chapter

245 Waterman Street, Suite 306, Providence, RI 02906

(401) 421-0008

Enroll by phone by calling toll-free **1-888-572-8566** (24 hours a day,
every day) with complete credit card information.

Log onto *www.medicalert.org/safereturn* to **enroll online.**

**

COMFORT ZONE

Comfort Zone is a web-based service that works with a variety of location devices to monitor the whereabouts of an individual with Alzheimer's. It is a full service application with 24-hour support *that allows family members to check on a person with Alzheimer's, no matter where they are in the country.* Those enrolled will also be enrolled in the MedicAlert/Safe Return Program.

For more information or to enroll in Comfort Zone, visit
www.alz.org/comfortzone or call 1-877-259-4850.

ELDER/ADULT POLICE ALERT REGISTRATION

Alzheimer's disease causes millions of Americans to lose their ability to recognize familiar places and faces. Many people cannot even remember their name or address. They may become disoriented and lost in their neighborhood or far from home.

It is common for a person with Alzheimer's disease to wander, many repeatedly, during the disease process. This behavior can be dangerous, even life threatening to individuals and stressful for caregivers. It is a known fact that elders and adults with Alzheimer's disease, other types of dementia, or medical conditions causing confusion may wander away from even the most caring of environments. Law-enforcement officials are keenly aware of the need to act swiftly to find these individuals and return them to safety.

As a result, the "Elder/Adult Police Alert Registration" form was the creation of Northwest Links, a collaboration of social service agencies in the Northwest corner of Rhode Island. In partnership with police departments in this area and the RI Chapter of the Alzheimer's Association, this group identified the information families could provide to their local police department to create a profile of persons at risk of wandering. Along with a recent photo, the information on this form is designed to save precious time in launching the search.

To acquire a registration form, contact:

> The Alzheimer's Association— Rhode Island Chapter
> (401) 421-0008
>
> or
>
> The Law Office of Laura M. Krohn
> (401) 398-8383

LUNCH AND LEARN

The Alzheimer's Association—Rhode Island Chapter offers two workshops that can be brought to the workplace during lunchtime for employers and employees. Caregivers are often stressed by their numerous responsibilities to family, work and caregiving and often have little spare time to attend informational meetings. These workshops were designed to enable caregivers to receive current up to date information to help them in their caregiving and hopefully reduce their level of stress.

The workshops are a free service of the Alzheimer's Association. The Lunch and Learn program is funded through a grant from the Rhode Island Department of Elderly Affairs.

Workshop 1: Maintain Your Brain

Launched in 2004, Maintain Your Brain™ is a public awareness program directed to 77 million American baby boomers. The workshop is reaching out to change the way the nation thinks about brain health, memory, healthy aging and Alzheimer's disease. Learning ways to keep your brain healthier as you age might also reduce your risk of Alzheimer's disease or other forms of dementia.

Workshop 2: Workplace 101-Alzheimer's Disease

This presentation is targeted to individuals who wish to learn more about Alzheimer's disease. Using brain images, it illustrates the difference between Alzheimer's and normal aging and how Alzheimer's affects the brain. Other sections explain the warning signs, how to get a diagnosis, key services offered by the Alzheimer's Association and hopeful advances in research.

Other Community Based Educational Programs Available

To sign up for a workshop or to find out more, contact the Alzheimer's Association—Rhode Island Chapter at (401) 421-0008.

The following books are highly recommended to those who are caring for loved ones affected by Alzheimer's disease and/or those who are simply seeking more information.

Learning to Speak Alzheimer's

A Groundbreaking Approach for Everyone Dealing
with the Disease

By Joanne Koenig Coste

The 36-Hour Day

A Family Guide To Caring For Persons with Alzheimer's Disease,
Related Dementia Illnesses and Memory Loss in Later Life

By Nancy L. Mace, M.A., and Peter V. Rabins, M.D., M.P.H.

Voices of Alzheimer's

Courage, Humor, Hope, and Love in the Face of Dementia

By Betsy Peterson

There's Still a Person in There

The Complete Guide to Treating and Coping with Alzheimer's

By Michael Castleman, Dolores Gallagher-Thompson, Ph.D.,
and Matthew Naythons, M.D.

What's Happening to Grandpa?

(A Children's Book)

By Maria Shriver

Talking to Alzheimer's

Simple Ways to Connect When You Visit with a Family Member or Friend

By Claudia J. Strauss

Losing My Mind

An Intimate Look at Life with Alzheimer's

By Thomas DeBaggio

Speaking Our Minds

Personal Reflections from Individuals with Alzheimer's

By Lisa Snyder, LCSW

What To Do When The Doctor Says

It's Early-Stage Alzheimer's

All the Medical, Lifestyle, and Alternative Medicine Information You Need to Stay Healthy and Prevent Progression

By Todd E. Feinberg, M.D. and Winnie Yu

My Journey into Alzheimer's Disease

Helpful Insights for Family and Friends

A True Story

By Robert Davis

Notes

CHRONIC
DISEASE
RESOURCES

ARTHRITIS: The Arthritis Foundation

2348 Post Road, Suite 204

Warwick, RI 02886

Phone: (401) 739-3773

www.arthritis.org

Call for information and programs that are designed to help those with arthritis live active lives through exercise, self-help, and support programs.

DIABETES: American Diabetes Association

222 Richmond Street

Providence, RI 02903

Phone: (401) 351-1674

www.diabetes.org

DIABETES: The Diabetes Resource Center

21 Peace Street

Providence, RI 02907

Phone: (401) 456-4419

www.diabetes.org

The Diabetes Resource Center at St. Joseph Hospital addresses the needs of high risk diabetes patients, including the uninsured, under-insured, and homeless.

They help with crisis intervention, medication, medical supplies, case managements, and education.

DOWN SYNDROME: The Down Syndrome Society of RI

99 Bald Hill Road

Cranston, RI 02920

Phone: (401) 463-5751

www.dssri.org

MUSCULAR DYSTROPHY:
The Muscular Dystrophy Association

931 Jefferson Boulevard, #1005

Warwick, RI 02886

Phone: (401) 732-1910

The Muscular Dystrophy Association provides financial assistance for wheelchairs, leg braces, and communication devices. It also runs an equipment loan program and transportation to and from its clinic.

PARKINSON DISEASE
Rhode Island Chapter of the American Parkinson Disease Association (APDA)

Phone: (401) 823-5700

www.riapda.org

The APDA serves the patients and caregivers of Rhode Island through the Information and Referral Center at Kent Hospital. They also offer support groups, education, and socialization.

For information regarding Alzheimer's Disease and Multiple Sclerosis, please see the Chapters in this Guide dedicated to those Chronic Diseases.

MULTIPLE SCLEROSIS SOCIETY

RHODE ISLAND CHAPTER

ABOUT THE RHODE ISLAND CHAPTER

**National
Multiple Sclerosis
Society**

The mission of the National Multiple Sclerosis (MS) Society is to end the devastating effects of Multiple Sclerosis. Founded in 1946, the National MS Society supports more research and serves more people with MS than any national voluntary MS organization in the world. Since its founding, over $280 million has been invested in research to find the cause, treatments and cure for MS. The National MS Society is also the only national voluntary MS organization that meets the standards of all major agencies that rate the fiscal responsibility of non-profit groups.

The National MS Society, RI Chapter, is one of 59 chapters across the United States that are helping advance the Society's mission: to end the devastating effects of MS. Founded in 1953, the Rhode Island Chapter is a non-profit organization and meets all the standards of the National Charities Information Bureau. The chapter provides services and programs to approximately 21,000 people affected by MS throughout Rhode Island.

Multiple Sclerosis is a chronic, often disabling disease of the central nervous system. Symptoms may be mild such as numbness in the limbs, or severe – paralysis or loss of vision. Most people with MS are diagnosed between the ages of 20 and 40 but the unpredictable physical and emotional effects can last a lifetime. The progress, severity and specific symptoms of MS in any one person cannot be predicted, but advances in research and treatment are giving hope to those affected by the disease.

Multiple sclerosis affects nearly a third of a million people in the US and a new case is diagnosed every hour. MS strikes more women than men. It is neither fatal, contagious nor inherited; the cause is not known yet. Today, exciting research and new treatments offer hope and improve the quality of life for people with the disease.

The Rhode Island Chapter fulfills their mission by helping keep families together despite the strain of dealing with chronic illness, helping people with MS get and keep jobs, providing accurate and up-to-date information about MS, giving free counseling, running self-help groups, advocating for people with disabilities, referring people to medical professionals with expertise in the disease, and in every way encouraging empowerment. For thousands of people with MS, these things mean the difference between living a full and active life and just existing.

The National Multiple Sclerosis Society is proud to be a source of information about Multiple Sclerosis. To contact the Rhode Island Chapter, please call (401) 738-8383 or toll free 1-800-FIGHT-MS.

**National
Multiple Sclerosis
Society**

Rhode Island Chapter

205 Hallene Road, Suite 209

Warwick, RI 02886

Phone: (401) 738-8383

www.NationalMSSociety.org/RIR

THE BOSTON HOME

2049 Dorchester Avenue

Boston, MA 02124

Phone: (617) 825-3905

www.TheBostonHome.org

In 1881, Miss Cordelia Harmon, a trained nurse, started The Boston Home for permanently disabled persons who could not be cared for in their homes nor accommodated in area hospitals. Since the inception, high standards of compassion and care have been sustained by generous donations of time and funds– and the vital commitment of wonderful staff and volunteers.

The mission of The Boston Home is to meet the long-term health care and related service needs of physically disabled adults in an environment that fosters self-determination. The Boston Home has a distinct niche in the nursing home industry as a progressive long-term facility for adult residents with physical disabilities. This non-profit community specializes in caring for adults, primarily age 40-60, with advanced Multiple Sclerosis and other progressive neurological diseases.

For The Boston Home residents, facing their disabilities is an ongoing challenge. They experience devastating changes such as loss of independence and control over their lives; poor self-esteem; and functional losses in mobility, coordination, cognition, vision, and speech. And because these changes can be variable, unpredictable, and progressive, The Boston Home residents never know what tomorrow may bring. Consequently, they are forced to confront these losses at many times during the course of their lives -- starting at diagnosis and again at each exacerbation -- as they require additional care. Many also suffer from fatigue and loss of

243

short-term memory. Residents learn that adjusting to MS is an continuous process and a constant battle against stress, fear, anxiety, anger, and depression.

At The Boston Home, residents are encouraged to work toward improving their quality of life by engaging in activities geared toward their interests and gaining support from each other. Residents are empowered by the technologies offered in The Boston Home's computer center, and often use e-mail and video-conferencing to communicate with friends and family. Many residents belong to The Boston Home organizations that meet on a regular basis. These groups include the Writing Group, where they can creatively explore their emotions and writing talents in a non-threatening environment; the Men's Discussion Group for men to share their viewpoints and even have heated debates on topics of interest; and the Resident Council, where residents can provide feedback on certain aspects of their care at The Boston Home. In addition to structured groups and hobbies, recreational activities such as poker games and cocktail hours promote social interaction.

Despite the disruption of their family and career goals due to illness, most of The Boston Home residents continue to realign their goals and face the ongoing challenges with dignity. The Boston Home residents are a remarkable group of individuals who work together with their peers and The Boston Home staff to live their lives to the fullest in a community-oriented environment.

For admissions information, contact Norma Harrington at

(617) 825-3905 *300.

Living with Multiple Sclerosis ("MS")
—The Voice of Pamela Luebeck—

After suffering from problems with visual acuity and keeping her balance, Pamela Luebeck sought medical attention for an evaluation. Through process of elimination and within a year of Pamela's first onset of symptoms, she was diagnosed at the young age of nineteen with intermittent exacerbated Multiple Sclerosis.

Pamela was treated with short doses of steroids and was able to finish college. After graduation, she went to work caring for disabled children. She experienced recurring vision problems, which she kept under control for a good period of time with steroid use. However, due to an extended amount of time off for treatment, Pamela eventually lost her job.

Thereafter Pamela lived at home with her parents, David and Verna Luebeck, while she underwent further testing. Pamela's parents cared for her intently during this time.

Luckily, Pamela's MS went into remission and she was able to move to Connecticut, where she purchased her own home and worked at a children's home as a child care supervisor and service coordinator. There in Connecticut she resided for twenty years, experiencing few medical problems.

One day while driving she started to experience vision problems and after having to pull over, she was rushed to the hospital in an ambulance. Doctors prescribed her new medication and again withdrew her driving privileges.

Unable to withstand the strain of the disease, her marriage failed. With the divorce came much stress which further induced Pamela's poor health conditions. Her MS worsened catastrophically.

In 2007, Pamela was transferred from a nursing home in Connecticut, to Saint Elizabeth's Home in East Greenwich for rehabilitation. Having Pamela in Rhode Island made more sense, since this was where her support system was.

After several years of being bounced between assisted living, hospital care, and nursing homes, Pamela now resides at Riverview Healthcare Center and she has finally found a "home".

"I think it's hard for people outside of a nursing home environment to deal with people like me, living with multiple sclerosis. We're a piece of work!" Pamela jokes. Pamela says she is doing "okay" now. "I have good days and I have bad days," she tells me. "Sometimes, I feel tired and I just need to rest. Living with multiple sclerosis has been frustrating and highly emotional."

Finding the appropriate support for her psychological issues has always been difficult for Pamela. Not many doctors or counselors make house calls today; at least not on a regular basis.

"Pamela is in a sort of doughnut hole", explains her attorney, Laura Krohn. "She is too healthy (and very young) to be the right candidate at nursing home, yet she has difficulty with movement (hence the nature of MS) so her ability to continue residing at an assisted living residence is uncertain. I do think The Boston Home is a right fit for Pam, but she is still somewhat ambulatory, so she is not a candidate for there either."

"The toughest part of Pamela's case has nothing to do with her legal issues; it is the non-legal issues such as the emotional stress and frustration in coordinating the appropriate care that Pam and her parents deal with every day", Attorney Krohn explains.

There is no special housing program for individuals with MS, which is why Pamela rehabilitated in a nursing home among seniors. If Pamela were non-ambulatory (completely unable to move without the aid of a wheelchair), she would be a candidate for the Boston Home, which is a care facility specifically for those with the disease.

Understandably, Pamela seems to have lost much self-esteem and says it is hard to ask for help. Her social worker explains that the best way to help Pam is to listen and be supportive.

While there are things Pamela can no longer do, like driving, the thing she misses most is her friends. "I feel like I woke up from a coma and I never had a chance to make my own decisions." Although she understands that her parents want the best for her, Pamela has a hard time living co-dependently. She confesses that she sometimes feels like a five-year old child again.

When I asked Pamela what advice she might give to others who could relate to her story and life struggle, she responded that people should "stick with it, no matter what! Don't be afraid to ask for help." She admits that she often has trouble following her own advice.

Pamela knows she is very fortunate to have the unwavering support of her parents and for this she says she is forever grateful. Although she is scared about her uncertain future, Pamela's wish is to someday live independently again. She has faith that someday, she just might.

Pamela Luebeck, 2008

Notes

CAREGIVER
SUPPORT
GROUPS

ALWAYS CALL FIRST TO CONFIRM
TIME AND DATE

Laura M. Krohn, Elder Law Attorney

Senior Resource Clinic

631 Main Street

East Greenwich, RI 02818

Phone: (401) 398-8383

Every Thursday: 6:00-8:00pm

www.seniorguideri.com

Hope Alzheimer's Center

25 Brayton Avenue

Cranston, RI 02920

Phone: (401) 946-9220

2nd Wednesday: 2:30-4:00pm

www.HopeAlzheimersCenter.org

*Adult Day Care Provided

RI Mood & Memory Clinic

1018 Waterman Avenue

East Providence, RI 02914

Phone: (401) 435-8950

4th Monday: 1:30pm

www.RIMMRI.com

*Adult Day Care Provided

Dora C. Howard Adult Day Center

715 Putnam Pike

Greenville, RI 02828

Phone: (401) 949-3890

4th Wednesday: 1:00-3:00pm

www.DoraCHoward.com

Beechwood House

10 Beach Street

North Kingstown, RI 02852

Phone: (401) 268-1590

3rd Tuesday: 2:30-4:00pm

Salvatore Mancini Center

2 Atlantic Boulevard

North Providence, RI 02911

Phone: (401) 553-1031 *1095

1st Wednesday: 10:30-11:30am

Leon Mathieu Senior Center

420 Main Street

Pawtucket, RI 02860

Phone: (401) 722-3560 * 352

4th Wednesday: 5:30pm

Johnston Senior Center

Johnston, RI

Phone: (401) 944-3343

3rd Wednesday: 1:30-2:30pm

Lincoln Senior Center

Lincoln, RI

Phone: (401) 723-3270

3rd Thursday: 10:30am

Newport Hospital

Newport, RI

Phone: (401) 848-4119

4th Thursday: 5:00-6:00pm

Coventry Senior Center

Coventry, RI

Phone: (401) 822-9178

1st Tuesday: 6:30pm

South Kingstown Senior Center

South Kingstown, RI

Phone: (401) 783-0960

2nd Wednesday: 1:15-2:45pm

Portsmouth Senior Center

110 Bristol Ferry Road

Portsmouth, RI 02871

Phone: (401) 683-4106

Every Tuesday: 9:30am

www.PortsmouthRI.com/SrCtr.htm

VNS of Newport & Bristol

1184 East Main Road

Portsmouth, RI 02871

Phone: (401) 682-2100

2nd Thursday: 6:30pm

www.VNSRI.com

Alzheimer's Association—Rhode Island Chapter Office

245 Waterman St., Suite 306 Room 506

Providence, RI 02906

Phone: (401) 421-0008

1st Tuesday: 6:30-8:00pm

Baptist Church of Warren

Warren, RI 0

Phone: (401) 396-5200

4th Wednesday: 6:30pm

Odyssey Health Care

Warwick, RI

Phone: (401) 738-1492

3rd Thursday: 4:30-5:30pm

Westerly Adult Day Services

65 Wells Street

Westerly, RI 02891

Phone: (401) 596-1336

2nd Tuesday: 7:00pm

Alternative Adult Care

84 Social Street

Woonsocket, RI 02895

Phone: (401) 766-0516

1st Wednesday: 10:00am

Eleanor Slater Hospital-Zambarano Unit

Burrillville, RI

Phone: (401) 567-5460

Last Thursday: 1:00pm

TIPS FOR CAREGIVERS

- Pay attention to your own health. Take leisure time for yourself. Acknowledge fatigue and take care of it.

- Utilize the resources available to assist you. Accept help when it is offered to you.

- Get support by attending support group meetings.

- Be realistic about what you can do. Don't be afraid to acknowledge that your loved one's needs may be beyond your ability.

- Be certain your loved one has executed the proper documents, giving you the authority to handle his/her financial and medical affairs.

- Have a contingency plan in place in the event that there is an emergency or a drastic change in health of your loved one or yourself.

WEECOPAUG, RHODE ISLAND
© GERI BOSCALIA CRITZ, *CLINICAL LABORATORY SCIENTIST, RI HOSPITAL*

*"THE MOST SATISFYING THING IN LIFE
IS TO HAVE BEEN ABLE TO GIVE A LARGE PART
OF ONE'S SELF TO OTHERS."*

Windsor Gallery Room at Highland Court

101 Highland Avenue

Providence, RI 02906

Phone: (401) 725-5962

2nd Wednesday: 7:00pm-9:00pm

❋

Bear Hill Village

156 Bear Hill Road

Cumberland, RI 02864

Phone: (401) 333-7972

3rd Wednesday: 7:00pm-9:00pm

❋

Dare to Dream

Immaculate Conception Church Parish Center

237 Garden Hills Drive

Cranston, RI 02920

Phone: (401) 944-3949

1st & 3rd Tuesday: 10:00am-11:30am

Hopkinton Police Station

406 Woodville Road

Hopkinton, RI 02804

Phone: (401) 491-9270

Last Monday: 10:30am-12:00pm

❈

In Touch

(A telephone support group for people

at home or in a long-term care facility)

Phone: (401) 738-8383

3rd Monday: 11:00am-12:00pm

❈

Key Club

Greenwood Community Church

805 Main Avenue

Warwick, RI 02886

Phone: (401) 826-9988

1st Wednesday: 11:30am-1:30pm

❈

MS Outlook

Warwick Public Library

600 Sandy Lane

Warwick, RI 02889

Phone: (401) 886-5827

3rd Tuesday:7:00pm-9:00pm

Notes

Notes

GOVERNMENT RESOURCE LISTINGS

RHODE ISLAND DEPARTMENT OF ELDERLY AFFAIRS (DEA)

35 Howard Avenue

Benjamin Rush Building 55

Cranston, RI 02920

(401) 462-3000

www.dea.state.ri.us

The DEA Home and Community Care Programs: These programs provide eligible seniors with innovative options to help them remain in the community and avoid premature institutionalization. These options are designed to assist the functionally impaired senior meet a wide variety of medical, environmental, and social needs. Based on eligibility, these programs may provide home health aide services, adult day services, a personal emergency response system, Meals on Wheels, Senior Companion, minor home modifications or minor assistive devices. If appropriate, placement in an assisted living facility may be made. For most programs, a person must be 65 or older, a resident of Rhode Island, and be basically homebound (unable to leave home without considerable assistance). For some persons on Medicaid, services may be provided at no charge. Others may have to make a contribution towards services.

For more information, call **(401) 462-0570.**

Case Management: Case management programs assist older Rhode Islanders who wish to remain at home for as long as possible. To qualify, Rhode Island residents must be aged 60 or older (or Alzheimer's victims of any age), homebound, frail or disabled and unable to remain at home without supportive care. Through case management services, clients receive an assessment of their needs. A case manager develops a plan of care which includes options for community based services. The case manager will assist in securing needed services, monitor the care plan, and offer training and   support for family caregivers. Clients with limited incomes and few cash resources may qualify for free or reduced-cost home care   services. For more information contact your nearest agency.

Aquidneck Island:	**Child/Family Service of Newport County** **(401) 845-2270**
East Bay:	**East Bay Community Action** **(401) 437-1000**
Kent County:	**Westbay Community Action** **(401) 732-4660**
Northern RI:	**C.R.A. Inc.** **(401) 822-6208**
Northwest:	**Ti-Town Community Action** **(401) 351-2750**
Providence County:	**Meals on Wheels of RI** **(401) 351-6700**
South County/ Coventry:	**C.R.A. Inc.** **(401) 822-6208**

State of Rhode Island
Department of Elderly Affairs

Senior Citizen Identification (ID) Cards: DEA issues cards to Rhode Islanders aged 60 and older and residents age 18-59 with a disability. These photo-identification cards contain the owner's name, address, date of birth, and signature. They are valid as proof of identification for cashing checks and other banking transactions involving government funds under $750 at Rhode Island financial institutions. ID cards are valid for five years from the date of issue and are issued weekdays at the DEA office from 9am-3pm. Seniors must present proof of age, such as a driver's license, birth certificate, or a RIPTA bus pass. Persons with a disability must present a current Social Security disability or Veteran Administration disability award letter. Two forms of verification are required for a DEA identification card. There is a $2 fee for a card. Additional information about the identification card program is available by calling DEA at **(401) 462-4000.**

The Rhode Island Registry of Motor Vehicles offers **free** identification cards to persons 59 and older. Office hours are 8:30am-4:00pm, Monday through Friday. For information, call **(401) 722-4407.**

State of Rhode Island
Department of Elderly Affairs

 # RHODE ISLAND DEPARTMENT OF HUMAN SERVICES (DHS)

www.dhs.state.ri.us

Rhode Island has a large number of elderly citizens, many of whom may require assistance at some point to maintain or enhance their quality of life. The Department of Human Services provides the following services to eligible elderly Rhode Islanders.

Medical Assistance Program: Medical Assistance is available for individuals over age 65 who are medically and financially eligible.

Long Term Care: Long Term Care services are available for adults over age 65 who require home or community based services. Institutional care is available if care at home or in the community is not possible.

Call a DHS long term care office for information about Medical Assistance (Medicaid) and nursing home care.

Area offices include:

Cranston:	(401) 462-5182	
East Providence:	(401) 222-7311	
Newport:	(401) 849-6000	
Providence:	(401) 462-2400	(Nursing Home Unit)
Providence:	(401) 222-7371	(Waiver/Adult Services)
Woonsocket:	(401) 235-6300	

Food Stamps: The Food Stamp Program provides supplemental food income for single or married individuals over age 60. Eligibility and the amount of the food stamp benefits depends on the size of your family, your income and other resources. Qualifying individuals get an ATM card that can be used to purchase food at most supermarkets.

Medicare Premium Payment Program: Rhode Islanders over age 65 who receive Medicare may qualify to have part or all of their deductible or co-payments for Medicare paid for by the state.

Title XX Homemaker Program: This program provides homemaker services and/or personal care assistance to individuals on Supplemental Security Income (SSI) who do not qualify for one of the Home and Community-Based Waiver programs.

SSI Assisted Living Program: This program provides enhanced Supplemental Security Income payments to Assisted Living Facilities for those individuals who require supervision in a residential setting.

Rhode Island Volunteer Guardianship Program Cornerstone Adult Services, Inc.

Cornerstone Adult Services

140 Warwick Neck Avenue

Warwick, Rhode Island 02889

Phone: (401) 739-5388

The RI Volunteer Guardianship Program is managed by Cornerstone Adult Services, Inc.. Guardianship is a legal arrangement through which the guardian is authorized to make certain decisions for another person, the Ward. The Volunteer Guardianship Program trains volunteers to help cognitively impaired elderly persons. Volunteers are appointed as Good Samaritan Guardians of the Ward by a Probate Court Judge and make important health care, residence and relationship decisions. Volunteer lawyers handle the court process for the proposed Guardian.

A person may be eligible to have a Volunteer Guardian if they are:

- At least 60 years of age.
- Medically determined to be cognitively impaired and need a surrogate decision maker
- Income meets requirements.
- Have no other available persons to act as Guardian.

Volunteer Guardians meet the following requirements:

- Receive initial training and ongoing training and support from the Volunteer Guardianship Program.

- Complete and Application for Volunteer Guardian.

- Are compassionate and caring people who come from all walks of life and backgrounds.

- Are both working and/or retired people.

For more information, to download forms, and to reserve seating for Guardianship classes, please call Patricia A. M. Vinci , Attorney at Law at (401) 739-2844 extension 36 or visit www.cornerstone-ri.com.

Notes

PRIVATE SENIOR RESOURCES

Rhode Island Assisted Living Association (RIALA)

2224 Pawtucket Avenue

East Providence, RI 02914

Phone: (401) 435-8888

Fax: (401) 435-8881

www.RIALA.org

RI Association of Facilities & Services for the Aging (RIAFSA)

225 Chapman Street, Box 7

Providence, RI 02906

Phone: (401) 490-7612

Fax: (401) 490-7614

www.RIAFSA.org

Rhode Island Partnership for Home Care (RIPHC)

334 East Avenue

Pawtucket, RI 02860

Phone: (401) 722– 9090

Fax: (401) 728-6509

www.RIPHC.org

Rhode Island Health Care Association (RIHCA)

57 Kilvert Street

Warwick, RI 02886

Phone: (401) 732-9333

www.RIHCA.com

Rhode Island Health Center Association (RIHCA)

235 Promenade Street, Suite 104

Providence, RI 02908

Phone: (401) 274-1771

Fax: (401) 274-1789

www.RIHCA.org

A Place for Mom

Phone: (877) 885-8583

A Place for Mom provides free comprehensive resources about senior housing and eldercare options to seniors and families in need.

A Place for Mom helps to provide options in the following areas:

- Independent and Assisted Living Communities
- Alzheimer's and Dementia Care
- Respite Care, Skilled Nursing Care, Home Care

Elizabeth Buffum Chace Center

Post Office Box 9476

Warwick, Rhode Island 02889

Business Phone: (401) 738-9700

Crisis Hotline: (401) 738-1700

Fax: (401) 738-1713

Advocacy, support and protection for victims of domestic violence.

AgeWell RI

Phone: (401) 223-2335

Or (866) 524-3935

Email: Agewellri.org; website: jsari.org

The Jewish Seniors Agency, Jewish Family Services, and the Jewish Community Center have collaborated to form AgeWell RI, a "virtual agency" that is now providing a single point of access to senior services.

Laura M. Krohn's Senior Resource Clinic

631 Main Street

East Greenwich, Rhode Island 02818

Phone: (401) 398-8383

www.seniorguideri.com

Visit the reception area and browse the valuable resource materials available to read or take home with you, from senior housing options, finding a realtor, reverse mortgage information, financial planners and accountant referrals, caregiver support group meetings and information, reading library.

Open and free to public

Notes

FUNERAL
PLANNING

PRE-ARRANGING AND PRE-PAYING FOR YOUR FUNERAL

There are many reasons to arrange and pay for your funeral in advance. Some clients want to provide comfort and peace of mind for family and friends. In a time of crisis, planning a funeral can be very stressful and emotional. Pre-paying also secures the price and cost of services against future increases.

Pre-paying for funeral services is also a very useful way to spend down assets to accelerate Medicaid eligibility for those who are receiving long-term care. This is because the purchase of a pre-paid funeral policy for the applicant or his/her spouse is a permitted transfer under the Rhode Island Medicaid rules. If purchasing a pre-paid funeral for this purpose, be sure that it is *irrevocable.*

The pre-paid funeral may include the cost of the casket, embalming services, cremation services, transportation to the cemetery, internment, and other related costs.

Many individuals have mixed feelings about planning for their funerals in advance. I can't blame them; I mean, who really wants to die, never mind plan for dying! Regardless of this fear, once it is done, every client feels a sense of relief that their family will have less stress, and security that their wishes will be carried out.

Of course, before signing and conveying any money on any contract, it is wise to have it reviewed by an attorney. And, like any smart consumer, look for the best service and product for your money.

By Laura M. Krohn, Attorney at Law, Author

Note: For questions and consumer information on prearranging a funeral, or other funeral and burial/cremation information, contact the Rhode Island Funeral Directors Association at (401) 885-3760 or visit www.rifda.org.

Smith Funeral & Memorial Services
8 Schoolhouse Road
Warren, Rhode Island 02885
Phone: (401) 245-4999
www.CelebrateWithSmith.com

❀

George C. Lima Funeral Home, Inc.
367 High Street
Bristol, Rhode Island 02809
Phone: (401) 253-9594

❀

Sansone Funeral Home, Inc.
192 Wood Street
Bristol, Rhode Island 02809
Phone: (401) 253-7110
www.SansoneFuneralHome.com

❀

Wilbur-Romano Funeral Home
615 Main Street
Warren, Rhode Island 02885
Phone: (401) 245-6818
www.WilburRomano.com

If you are interested in purchasing an extra
copy, please visit us at
www.seniorguideri.com
or call (401) 398-8383

Carpenter-Jenks Quaker Lane Chapel
659 East Greenwich Avenue
West Warwick, Rhode Island 02893
Phone: (401) 826-1600
www.CarpenterJenks.com

❈

Gorton Funeral Home
721 Washington Street
Coventry, Rhode Island 02816
Phone: (401) 821-7306
www.GortonFuneralHome.com

❈

Frank Trainor & Sons Funeral Home Inc
982 Warwick Avenue
Warwick, Rhode Island 02888
Phone: (401) 461-4843

❈

Hill Funeral Home Inc
822 Main Street
East Greenwich, Rhode Island 02818
Phone: (401) 884-9222
www.HillFuneralHome.com

❈

Iannotti Funeral Home
415 Washington Street
Coventry, Rhode Island 02816
Phone: (401) 821-1100

❈

Peter J. Barrett Funeral Home
1328 Warwick Avenue
Warwick, Rhode Island 02888
Phone: (401) 463-9000

Potvin & Son Funeral Home Inc
45 Curson Street
West Warwick, Rhode Island 02893
Phone: (401) 821-6868

❋

Prata-Murphy Funeral Home
78 Providence Street
West Warwick, Rhode Island 02893
Phone: (401) 821-6760
www.MurphyFuneralHomes.org

❋

Henault Gallogly Funeral Home
5 Eddy Street
West Warwick, Rhode Island 02893
Phone: (401) 821-8484
www.GalloglyFuneralHome.com

❋

Russell J. Boyle & Son Funeral Home
142 Centerville Road
Warwick, Rhode Island 02886
Phone: (401) 732-8800
www.BoyleAndSonFuneralHome.com

❋

Thomas & Walter Quinn Funeral Home Inc
2435 Warwick Avenue
Warwick, Rhode Island 02889
Phone: (401) 738-1977
www.TheQuinnFuneralHome.com

Fern Acres Funeral Home
72 Willow Avenue
Little Compton, Rhode Island 02837
Phone: (401) 635-4757

❋

Hambley Funeral Home
30 Red Cross Avenue
Newport, Rhode Island 02840
Phone: (401) 846-0698
www.MemorialFuneralHome.com

❋

Connors Funeral Home
55 West Main Road
Portsmouth, Rhode Island 02871
Phone: (401) 683-2511
www.MemorialFuneralHome.com

❋

Memorial Funeral Home
375 Broadway
Newport, Rhode Island 02840
Phone: (401) 846-0350
www.MemorialFuneralHome.com

❋

O'Neill-Hayes Funeral Home
465 Spring Street
Newport, Rhode Island 02840
Phone: (401) 846-0932
www.ONHFH.com

❋

Pocasset Memorial Funeral Home, Inc.
462 Main Road
Tiverton, Rhode Island 02878
Phone: (401) 625-5945
www.Almeida-Pocasset.com

A. A. Mariani & Son, Inc.
200 Hawkins Street
Providence, Rhode Island 02904
Phone: (401) 861-5432
www.MarianiAndSon.com

❀

A. Tarro & Sons Funeral Home
425 Broadway
Providence, Rhode Island 02909
Phone: (401) 421-7971

❀

Anderson-Winfield Funeral Home, Inc.
605 Putnam Pike
Greenville, Rhode Island 02828
Phone: (401) 949-0180

❀

B. Maceroni & Sons Funeral Home, Inc.
1381 Smith Street
North Providence, Rhode Island 02911
Phone: (401) 353-2400
www.Maceroni.com

❀

Barry Stapleton Holdredge Funeral Home, Inc.
684 Park Avenue
Cranston, Rhode Island 02910
Phone: (401) 461-5050
www.CranstonFuneral.com

❀

Bell Funeral Home, Inc.
571 Broad Street
Providence, Rhode Island 02907
Phone: (401) 331-0200
www.BellFuneralHome.net

Bellows Funeral Chapel
160 River Road
Lincoln, Rhode Island 02865
Phone: (401) 723-9792
www.BellowsFH.com

❋

Boucher Funeral Home, Inc.
272 Sayles Avenue
Pascoag, Rhode Island 02859
Phone: (401) 568-5760

❋

Bright Funeral Home
290 Public Street
Providence, Rhode Island 02905
Phone: (401) 331-9411
www.Bright-FuneralHome.com

❋

Brown Funeral Homes, Inc.
1496 Victory Highway
Oakland, Rhode Island 02858
Phone: (401) 568-5500

❋

Butterfield Home and Chapel
500 Pontiac Avenue
Cranston, Rhode Island 02910
Phone: (401) 461-0151
www.TheButterfieldHome.com

❋

Charles Coelho Funeral Home, Inc.
151 Cross Street
Central Falls, Rhode Island 02863
Phone: (401) 724-9440
www.CoelhoFuneralHome.com

Cheetham Mortuary, Inc.
1012 Newport Avenue
Pawtucket, Rhode Island 02861
Phone: (401) 725-4525
www.CheethamMortuary.com

Corrigan-Brown Funeral Home, Inc.
1496 Victory Highway
Oakland, Rhode Island 02858
Phone: (401) 568-5500

Costigan-O'Neill Funeral Home, Inc.
220 Cottage Street
Pawtucket, Rhode Island 02860
Phone: (401) 723-4035
www.RIFunerals.com

Curtis J. Holt's & Sons
510 South Main Street
Woonsocket, Rhode Island 02895
Phone: (401) 769-0133

D. W. Bellows & Son
85 Park Place
Pawtucket, Rhode Island 02860
Phone: (401) 723-0084

www.BellowsFH.com

Darlington Mortuary Of L Heroux & Son, Inc.
1042 Newport Avenue
Pawtucket, Rhode Island 02861
Phone: (401) 722-4376

Egidio DePardo & Sons Funeral Home, Inc.
75 Harris Avenue
Woonsocket, Rhode Island 02895
Phone: (401) 762-3746

❀

Robbins Funeral Home, Inc.
2251 Mineral Spring Avenue
North Providence, Rhode Island 02911
Phone: (401) 231-9307
www.RobbinsFuneralHome.com

❀

Olson & Parent Funeral Home
417 Plainfield Street
Providence, Rhode Island 02909
Phone: (401) 944-6460
www.OlsonParent.com

❀

Fournier & Fournier, Inc.
463 South Main Street
Woonsocket, Rhode Island 02895
Phone: (401) 769-0940

❀

Fournier & Fournier, Inc.
99 Cumberland Street
Woonsocket, Rhode Island 02895
Phone: (401) 769-0940

❀

Hoey-Arpin-Williams-King Funeral Home
168 Academy Avenue
Providence, Rhode Island 02908
Phone: (401) 272-6363
www.RIFuneral.com

J. H. Williams & Co. Funeral Home
210 Taunton Avenue
East Providence, Rhode Island 02914
Phone: (401) 434-2600

❋

J. J. Duffy Funeral Home, Inc.
757 Mendon Road
Cumberland, Rhode Island 02864
Phone: (401) 334-2300
www.JJDuffyFuneralHome.com

❋

James J. Gallogly & Sons Funeral Home, Inc.
671 Broad Street
Providence, Rhode Island 02907
Phone: (401) 331-7608
www.GalloglyFuneralHome.com

❋

Jones-Walton-Sheridan Funeral Home
1895 Broad Street
Cranston, Rhode Island 02905
Phone: (401) 781-1188
www.JWSFH.com

❋

Lachapelle Funeral Home, Inc.
643 Main Street
Pawtucket, Rhode Island 02860
Phone: (401) 724-2226

❋

Lauzon Funeral Home
185 Spring Street
Woonsocket, Rhode Island 02895
Phone: (401) 769-2537

Lincoln Funeral Home, Inc.
1501 Lonsdale Avenue
Lincoln, Rhode Island 02865
Phone: (401) 726-4117

❋

Manning-Heffern Funeral Home
68 Broadway
Pawtucket, Rhode Island 02860
Phone: (401) 723-1312
www.ManningHeffern.com

❋

Max Sugarman Memorial Chapel
458 Hope Street
Providence, Rhode Island 02906
Phone: (401) 331-8094

❋

Marino Pontarelli Funeral Home
971 Branch Avenue
Providence, Rhode Island 02904
Phone: (401) 331-7390

❋

McAloon & Kelly Funeral Home
643 Main Street
Pawtucket, Rhode Island 02860
Phone: (401) 722-1527

❋

Menard's Funeral Home
127 Carrington Avenue
Woonsocket, Rhode Island 02895
Phone: (401) 762-1825

Menard's Funeral Home
71 Central Street
Manville, Rhode Island 02838
Phone: (401) 762-1825

�֎

Merrick R. Williams Funeral Home
530 Smithfield Avenue
Pawtucket, Rhode Island 02860
Phone: (401) 723-2042
www.MerrickRWilliamsFH.com

✷

Monahan, Kelly, Drabble & Sherman Funeral Home
230 Waterman Street
Providence, Rhode Island 02906
Phone: (401) 331-4592
www.MKDS.com

✷

Nardolillo Funeral Home, Inc.
1278 Park Avenue
Cranston, Rhode Island 02910
Phone: (401) 942-1220
www.NardolilloFH.com

✷

Pennine Funeral Home, Inc.
28 Grove Street
Providence, Rhode Island 02909
Phone: (401) 421-7739
www.PennineFuneralHome.com

✷

Perry-McStay Funeral Home, Inc.
2555 Pawtucket Avenue
East Providence, Rhode Island 02914
Phone: (401) 434-3885

Peter Kubaska & Son Funeral Home, Inc.
35 Harris Avenue
Woonsocket, Rhode Island 02895
Phone: (401) 762-0220

❋

Rebello Funeral Home, Inc.
901 Broadway
East Providence, Rhode Island 02914
Phone: (401) 434-7744
www.RebelloFuneralHome.com

❋

Robbins Funeral Home
2251 Mineral Spring Avenue
Providence, Rhode Island 02911
Phone: (401) 231-9307
www.RobbinsFuneralHome.com

❋

Romano & Sons Funeral Home
627 Union Avenue
Providence, Rhode Island 02909
Phone: (401) 944-5151

❋

Romenski & Son, Inc.
342 High Street
Central Falls, Rhode Island 02863
Phone: (401) 722-7250

❋

Russell J. Boyle & Son Funeral Homes
331 Smith Street
Providence, Rhode Island 02908
Phone: (401) 272-3100
www.BoyleAndSonFuneralHome.com

Shalom Memorial Chapel
1100 New London Avenue
Cranston, Rhode Island 02920
Phone: (401) 463-7771

✳

Sinai Mount Memorial Chapel
825 Hope Street
Providence, Rhode Island 02906
Phone: (401) 331-3337
www.DignityMemorial.com

✳

Skeffington Funeral Home
925 Chalkstone Avenue
Providence, Rhode Island 02908
Phone: (401) 331-3900
www.SkeffingtonFuneralHome.com

✳

Smith–Mason Funeral Home, Inc.
398 Willett Avenue
East Providence, Rhode Island 02915
Phone: (401) 433-2300

✳

Tucker-Quinn Funeral Home, Inc.
649 Putnam Pike
Greenville, Rhode Island 02828
Phone: (401) 949-1370
www.TuckerquinFuneralHome.com

✳

William W. Tripp Funeral Home
1008 Newport Avenue
Pawtucket, Rhode Island 02861
Phone: (401) 722-2140
www.TrippFuneralHome.com

289

Winfield & Sons Funeral Home & Crematory, Inc.
Route 116
Scituate, Rhode Island 02857
Phone: (401) 647-5421
www.WinfieldAndSons.com

❉

Woodlawn Funeral Home
600 Pontiac Avenue
Cranston, Rhode Island 02910
Phone: (401) 421-0289
www.WoodlawnGattone.com

❉

W. Raymond Watson Funeral Home
350 Willett Avenue
Riverside, Rhode Island 02915
Phone: (401) 433-4400
www.WRWatsonFuneralHome.com

BLOCK ISLAND, RHODE ISLAND
© GERI BOSCALIA CRITZ, *CLINICAL LABORATORY SCIENTIST, RI HOSPITAL*

Avery Storti Funeral Service
88 Columbia Street
Wakefield, Rhode Island 02879
Phone: (401) 783-7271

Buckler-Johnston Funeral Home
121 Main Street
Westerly, Rhode Island 02891
Phone: (401) 596-2465

Cranstons Of Wickford Funeral Home, Inc.
140 West Main Street
North Kingstown, Rhode Island 02852
Phone: (401) 294-4013

Forbes Funeral Home Inc
28 Columbia Street
Wakefield, Rhode Island 02879
Phone: (401) 789-6550

Gaffney-Dolan Funeral Home Inc
59 Spruce Street
Westerly, Rhode Island 02891
Phone: (401) 596-2648

Lawrence E. Jr. Fagan Funeral Home
825 Boston Neck Road
North Kingstown, Rhode Island 02852
Phone: (401) 295-5603
www.TheQuinnFuneralHome.com

Nardollilo Funeral Home
1111 Boston Neck Road
Narragansett, RI 02882
Phone: (401) 789-6300
www.NardolilloFH.com

Rushlow-Iacoi Funeral Home
64 Friendship Street
Westerly, Rhode Island 02891
Phone: (401) 596-2352
www.RushlowIacoiFuneralHome.com

S. R. Avery Funeral Home
2A Bank Street
Hope Valley, Rhode Island 02832
Phone: (401) 539-2271

If you are interested in purchasing an extra
copy, please visit us at
www.seniorguideri.com

Notes

GLOSSARY

Adult Day Care

Adult day care is a planned program of activities designed to promote well-being though social and health related services. Adult day care centers operate during daytime hours in a safe, supportive environment. Nutritious meals that accommodate special diets are typically included, along with an afternoon snack.

Adult day care centers can be public or private, non-profit or for-profit. The intent of an adult day center is primarily two-fold:

- To provide older adults an opportunity to get out of the house and receive both mental and social stimulation

- To give caregivers a much-needed break in which to attend to personal needs, or simply rest and relax

Good candidates for adult day care are individuals who can benefit from the friendship and functional assistance a day care center offers or that may be physically or cognitively challenged but do not require 24-hour supervision.

Adult day dare center participants need to be mobile, with the possible assistance of a cane, walker or wheelchair, and in most cases, they must also be continent.

Common recreational activities include arts and crafts, musical entertainment, mental stimulation games, exercise, discussion groups, holiday and birthday celebrations, local outings, and inter-generational programs.

Besides recreational activities, some adult day care centers provide transportation to and from the center, social services including counseling and support groups for caregivers, and health support services such as blood pressure monitoring and vision screening. Often, Adult Day Care Centers provide health assessments and therapy if staffed with an RN and other health professionals. Other types of day care provide social and health services specifically for individuals with Alzheimer's (including earl-onset) or a related type of dementia.

The cost for an adult day care center ranges but is typically set on a per-day basis. Many facilities offer services on a sliding fee scale, meaning that what you pay is based on your income and ability to pay. Be sure to ask about financial assistance.

Payment options will depend on the individual's situation, and may include private-pay, long-term care insurance, Medicare and Medicaid.

Assisted Living

An assisted living residence provides care for seniors who need some help with activities of daily living yet wish to remain as independent as possible. Essentially, assisted living is the middle ground between independent living and nursing homes. The goal of assisted living is to provide seniors with an environment that encourages as much autonomy as they are capable of, while providing socialization, safety, and family peace of mind. Most residences offer 24-hour supervision and an array of support services, with more privacy, space, and dignity than many nursing homes, and at a lower cost.

Assisted Living Residences are also called personal care homes, residential care facilities, domiciliary care, sheltered housing, and community residences.

An Assisted Living Residence helps seniors with personal care/custodial care, such as bathing, dressing, toileting, eating, grooming and transport.

Daily contact with supervisory staff is the defining characteristic of an Assisted Living Residence. Medical care is usually limited in an Assisted Living Residence, but it is possible to contract for other medical needs.

Assisted Living Residences are owned and operated by both for-profit and non-profit organizations and can range in cost depending on where you live. Fees may be inclusive or there may be additional charges for special services.

Costs are generally lower than for full-time home health services or nursing home care. Payment options will depend on the individuals situation, and may include private-pay, long-term care insurance, and Medicaid.

Geriatric Assessment

A geriatric assessment is a comprehensive evaluation designed to optimize an older person's ability to enjoy good health, improve their overall quality of life, reduce the need for hospitalization and/or institutionalization, and enable them to live independently for as long as possible.

Typically, the assessment is done by a team of experts which often include geriatricians, neurologists, social workers, therapists, dieticians, psychologists, pharmacists, and geriatric nurse practitioners.

Geriatric Care Manager

A geriatric care manager (GCM) is a professional with specialized knowledge and expertise in senior care issues. Ideally, a GCM holds an advanced degree in gerontology, social work, psychology, nursing, or a related health and human services field.

Sometimes called case managers, elder care managers, service coordinators or care coordinators, GCMs are individuals who evaluate your situation, identify solutions, and work with you to design a plan for maximizing your elder's independence and well being.

Geriatric care management usually involves an in-depth assessment, developing a care plan, arranging for services, and following up or monitoring care. While you are not obligated to implement any part of the suggested care plan, geriatric care managers often suggest potential alternatives you might not have considered, due to their experience and familiarity with community resources. They can also make sure your loved one receives the best possible care and any benefits to which they are entitled.

Geriatric Neurologist

As a Geriatric subspecialty, Geriatric Neurology focuses on neurological diseases and disorders that are common to older adults. The correct diagnosis of neurological disorders in older adults is difficult because signs of disease may mimic normal signs of aging. In addition, patients frequently have more than one neurological problem at a time. This subspecialty the result of growing recognition that neurological conditions may present differently in middle or late life, and that the older adult may require different treatments than younger patients.

One of the most common geriatric neurology problems is memory loss and dementia. In addition, many other neurological disorders are more common with age including, stroke, Parkinson's disease, seizures, and gait disorders. The subspecialty of geriatric neurology focuses on evaluating and treating these common neurological conditions in older adults.

Geriatric Physician

A Geriatrician is a medical doctor who specializes in the medical needs of seniors. All seniors should consult with a geriatrician, even if they already have a family physician.

Home Health Care

Home care typically refers to medical and/or non-medical services that assist individuals with daily living.

Home care is becoming an increasingly popular choice for care because it enables individuals to remain in their own environments longer and helps families better plan for the care of a loved one.

Many families utilize home care agencies to supplement the services they cannot perform themselves for a loved one due to work and other family commitments. These agencies provide an extra pair of hands and assist in the overall care management of a loved one.

Most agencies can provide services for as little as six hours a week up to 24 hours a day, seven days a week. The schedules are usually determined during the assessment process and vary depending on the needs of both the family caregiver and the needs of the client.

Caregivers need to be reminded that they are at health risk if they try to take on too much and forget to take care of themselves. *It is just as important that the caregiver is getting proper nutrition, rest, and exercise as it is for the person they are caring for.*

Hospice

Hospice represents a compassionate approach to end-of-life care. Hospice care is an option for people whose life expectancy is approaching six months or less. Hospice programs focus on all the aspects of life and well-being including the physical, social, emotional, and spiritual realms. There is no age restriction for hospice care and anyone in the last stages of life is eligible for the services. While some hospitals, nursing homes and other health care facilities provide hospice care onsite, hospice most often takes place in the comfort of your own home, allowing you to remain in familiar surroundings as you prepare for a meaningful life conclusion.

Hospice services are generally structured according to a person's specific needs which often change over time. A hospice team may include any combination of the following services: Nursing Care, Social Services, Physician Services, Spiritual Support and Counseling, Clergy and other spiritual services, Home Health Aides and Homemaker Services, Trained Volunteer Support, Physical, Occupational, and Speech, Respite Care, Inpatient Care, and Bereavement Support.

Independent Living

Independent Living provides the greatest versatility and freedom. Independent Living for seniors refers to residence in a compact, easy-to-maintain, private apartment or house within a community of other seniors. The housing arrangement is designed exclusively for seniors, generally those aged 55 and older.

Independent Living for seniors is also known as Retirement Communities, Retirement Homes, Senior Apartments, Senior Housing, and Independent Living Communities.

As the name implies, Independent Living is just that: the ability to maintain one's residence and lifestyle without custodial or medical assistance. If custodial or medical care becomes necessary, residents in Independent Living for seniors are permitted to bring in outside services of their choice. Some facilities even have a social worker on staff to assist in contacting agencies that provide medical or personal care. Many also are gated communities with their own security guards. Some senior apartment complexes provide community services such as recreational programs, transportation services, and meals in a communal dining room.

Medicaid

Medicaid is a federal-state partnership program which pays for about half of all long-term care costs in America. Medicaid eligibility is crucial for seniors who face the possibility of long-term nursing care.

Unlike Medicare, Medicaid is not an entitlement and eligibility is based on need (both medical and financial). The regulations that govern Medicaid eligibility are very complex and individuals should seek advice to navigate the rules and requirements properly.

Medicare

Medicare is a federal health insurance program for the elderly and the disabled. Medicare benefits are tied to Social Security benefits. The Medicare program consists of three parts: Medicare Part A which provides hospital insurance and skilled nursing insurance, Medicare Part B which provides medical insurance, and Medicare Part D which provides some coverage for prescription drugs. Unlike Medicaid, Medicare is an entitlement and is not based on financial need.

Respite Care

Respite care provides time off for family members or other caregivers who care for someone who is ill, injured or frail. It can take place in an adult day center, in the home of the person being cared for, or even in a residential setting such as an assisted living residence or nursing home.

Although there are different approaches to respite care, all have the same basic objective: to provide caregivers with planned temporary, intermittent, substitute care, allowing for relief from the daily responsibilities of caring for the care recipient. Respite care is essential for all caregivers in order to relieve stress and prevent burnout. For more information refer to the caregiver stress article in the support group section.

Senior Centers

Senior Centers are meeting places that are dedicated to helping seniors live meaningful lives of dignity, enjoyment and useful purpose. The centers' main focus is improving and enriching lives of seniors through programs, resources and volunteer work. They provide programs and services that enhance their social, physical and mental well-being.

Each town typically has its own Senior Center for the surrounding community. Membership fees vary for town and non-town members but prices are generally minimal. Most centers provide their own transportation.

Nursing Homes & Rehabilitation

A Nursing Home can provide custodial care and/or skilled nursing to provide 24 hour care to people who can no longer care for themselves due to physical, emotional, or mental conditions. A licensed physician supervises each patient's care and a nurse or other medical professional is almost always on the premises.

Skilled medical care includes services of trained professionals that are needed for a limited period of time following an injury or illness. This may include would care, I.V. administration and monitoring, physical therapy, speech therapy, occupational therapy, or administering and monitoring I.V. antibiotics for a severe infection. Skilled care may also be needed on a long term basis if a resident requires injections, ventilation or other similar treatment.

Custodial or personal care includes assistance with bathing, dressing, eating, grooming, transport, and incontinence care. This type of care may be a temporary or long-term need depending on the situation.

Nursing Homes and rehabilitation centers offer an array of services, in addition to the basic skilled nursing care and the custodial care. They provide a room (private or semi-private), all meals, some social activities, personal care, 24-hour nursing supervision and access to medical services when needed. In addition, many Nursing Homes provide respite care so that caregivers can have a break and interim medical care which is care after a hospital stay.

Support Group
A support group generally refers to a group of individuals who meet on a regular basis to exchange mutual support. They often focus on a shared area of difficulty, most often a disease or condition. Groups are organized at various locations but typically are facilitated by a social worker. Support groups are a crucial resource for caregivers because often the caregiver forgets to take care of him or herself while providing care and support to a loved one. In a support group environment, the caregiver can receive valuable support, advice, and resource information from other individuals familiar with the issues the caregiver is facing.

SHIPPING ADDRESS:

NAME:

COMPANY:

ADDRESS:

CITY: STATE: ZIP:

BOOK COST INCLUDING TAX   **$10.70/BK** =$

SHIPPING & HANDLING COST:
1-10BOOKS = $2.50
10-20BOOKS=$5.00
FOR LARGER ORDERS, PLEASE CALL 401-398-8383.

SHIPPING = $_____
TOTAL DUE =$

FOR TAX EXEMPT ORGANIZATIONS, PLEASE INCLUDE TAX EXEMPT NUMBER HERE: _____

PAYMENT TYPE: ☐CHECK   ☐CREDIT CARD   ☐MONEY ORDER
COMMENTS/SHIPPING INSTRUCTIONS:

BILLING INFORMATION: (IF DIFFERENT FROM ABOVE)

NAME:

ADDRESS:

CITY: STATE: ZIP:

SENIOR RESOURCE GUIDE OF RHODE ISLAND SPONSORS

THE FOLLOWING ARE THE SPONSORS OF THE SENIOR RESOURCE GUIDE. WITHOUT THESE SPONSORS, THE PRODUCTION AND DISTRIBUTION OF THIS CRUCIAL RESOURCE WOULD NOT HAVE BEEN POSSIBLE.

THANK YOU FOR YOUR SUPPORT TO:

WASHINGTON TRUST BANK

ATRIA HARBOR HILL RETIREMENT LIVING

EUCLID FINANCIAL

HEALTH TOUCH

RI KITCHEN & BATH

IF YOU WISH TO SPONSOR THE SENIOR RESOURCE GUIDE OF RHODE ISLAND, PLEASE EMAIL LAURA AT LAURA@LAURAKROHN.COM FOR INFORMATION.

EUCLID
FINANCIAL SERVICES LLC

At *Euclid Financial Services LLC*, our mission is to provide the highest quality of advice, service and education to our senior clients, their businesses and families.

Senior Retirement Planning

- Pension Evaluation
- Fund Allocation/Rebalancing
- 401(k) Rollover
- Income Planning
- Traditional/Roth IRA Planning
- RMD Calculation/ Solutions
- Medicaid Income Planning
- Estate Planning
- Trust Funding Solutions

One-on-One Personal Planning

- Life Insurance
- Long-Term Care Insurance
- Disability Insurance
- College/Education Planning
- Charitable Gifting Solutions
- Cash Flow Planning

Pre-Paid Funeral Funding Solutions

- Guaranteed Issue Life Insurance

372 Broadway, Suite D Pawtucket, RI 02860
Phone: 401-727-2727 Fax: 866-852-3661
Info@euclidadvisors.com
www.EuclidFinancialServices.com